UNDERSTANDING IRAs

Dearborn
Financial Institute, Inc.®

This publication is designed to provide accurate and authoritative information in regard to the subject matter covered. It is sold with the understanding that the publisher is not engaged in rendering legal, accounting or other professional service. If legal advice or other expert assistance is required, the services of a competent professional person should be sought.

This text is updated periodically to reflect changes in laws and regulations. To verify that you have the most recent update, you may call Dearborn at 1-800-423-4723.

©1998 by Dearborn Financial Publishing, Inc.®
Published by Dearborn Financial Institute, Inc.®

Printed in the United States of America.

First printing, April 1998

Library of Congress Cataloging-in-Publication Data

Understanding IRAs.
     p.   cm.
   ISBN 0–7931–2860–9 (pbk.)
   1. Individual retirement accounts– –United States.   2. Retirement
income– –United States.   I. Dearborn Financial Institute.
HG1660.U5U58   1998
   332.024'01– –dc21
                               98–15130
                                  CIP

⬛⬛⬛⬛⬛ Table of Contents

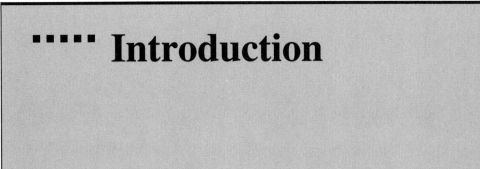

Introduction

ndividual retirement accounts (IRAs) have been the staple of retirement investing for over 20 years. Why? Because their special tax status increases the size of the nest egg investors can expect when they retire.

From the mid-'80s until 1998, however, the market for IRAs was stagnant. Restrictions on their use, brought in by the Tax Reform Act of 1986, limited the number of people who could take advantage of their full potential.

The Taxpayer Relief Act of 1997 changed that by expanding the universe of people eligible to take advantage of IRAs. Income limits on eligibility for deducting contributions to traditional IRAs were ratcheted up. And a new type of IRA—the Roth IRA—offered an attractive new savings opportunity.

In addition, changes in the restrictions on preretirement distributions from all IRAs make them a more flexible investment, easing fears of potential investors who don't want their money tied up and unavailable should a financial emergency arise.

For most people, the income from Social Security and employer retirement plans will not be sufficient to provide the resources they want after their working years end. For them, IRAs are, at least, the beginning of an answer.

This course is designed for financial representatives and insurance producers who want a better understanding of this important investment vehicle. Much confusion exists about who can establish an IRA, the amount that can be contributed, whether contributions can be deducted and how they can accumulate in their tax-preferred status. The purpose of this course is to clarify some of these complicated issues.

Once you understand IRAs, you'll be better prepared to help your clients meet their own retirement objectives. This material will help you explain to clients the advantages of many retirement-related investment opportunities.

Stephen D. Froikin, J.D.
Editor

1

IRAs and Personal Investment Strategies

I ndividual retirement accounts (IRAs) are among the most popular personal financial tools for working Americans. They benefit individuals in all income brackets. In fact, they may be the only tax shelter that millions of Americans with relatively modest incomes will ever use.

Insurance producers and financial practitioners who let clients and prospects know the privileges and responsibilities (as well as the many investment opportunities) that go along with IRA ownership provide a valuable service. Whether your main professional focus is insurance, securities, tax or financial planning, the information in this book will help you understand and explain IRAs better.

IRAs have undergone many changes since their introduction in 1974, but their fundamental purpose has remained the same: to provide tax-favored retirement savings for those who choose to use them. Recent law changes, however, have introduced new types of IRAs and increased their flexibility so they are not just for retirement anymore.

■ ■ ■ ■ ■

■ WHAT IS AN IRA?

An IRA is a special type of account set up to give investors a tax break when they save for retirement. Although there are many variations of the concept, the common thread is this: anyone may contribute up to $2,000 to an IRA each year toward their retirement. Every IRA has features that increase retirement savings by reducing the investor's taxes.

Exactly how this works depends on the type of IRA used. There are now two major types:

- traditional IRAs, which offer eligible investors a tax deduction when they contribute; and

- Roth IRAs, which offer no tax deduction, but allow tax-free withdrawals that are not possible with traditional IRAs.

In this chapter you will learn about the many advantages IRAs offer investors, the distinctions between different types of IRA and how IRA contributions may be invested.

■ ADVANTAGES OF IRAs

The advantages of IRAs are many and the drawbacks are few. In fact the biggest drawback of an IRA is that your clients are limited to contributing $2,000 a year to them.

Tax-Free Growth

Now that IRAs come in several varieties, it is important to understand that the one thing that makes all IRAs similar is the principle of tax-free growth. IRAs shelter interest, dividends and capital gains earnings realized in the IRA until their owners withdraw the money. This is true for a traditional IRA and it is true for the new Roth IRA. (It is also true of the special forms of IRA discussed in Chapter 6.)

Deductible Contributions or Tax-Free Withdrawals

Beyond tax-free growth, most IRAs offer one additional tax-savings feature that makes them very attractive investments. Before 1998, this feature was the ability to deduct contributions on the eligible IRA investor's tax return. This is still possible for traditional IRAs. But beginning in 1998, the alternative IRA—the Roth IRA—allows investors to forgo the deduction and instead take withdrawals tax free.

Now IRA investors have a choice: tax savings at the beginning, in the form of deductible contributions, or tax savings at the end, in the form of tax-free withdrawals. This text discusses the factors that might make one type of IRA better than another, but either way, these features coupled with tax-free growth make IRAs an attractive investment for your client.

Clients Control Their IRAs

Unlike other types of retirement investments, which may be under the control of an employer, IRAs are completely under the control of their owners. With the benefit of sound advice from their financial advisors, IRA owners decide how to invest the money contributed to the account. The owners can also decide whether to save IRA money for retirement or use it sooner (though penalties may apply for some IRA withdrawals by individuals under age 59½). No matter how often IRA owners change jobs, their IRAs are always in place. As a result, IRAs may be especially appropriate for your clients who change jobs frequently.

Annual Contributions Not Required

IRA owners don't have to make contributions to their IRAs every year if they don't want to or can't afford to. The IRS specifies maximum annual contribution limits

ILL. 1.1 ■ *IRAs—A Brief History*

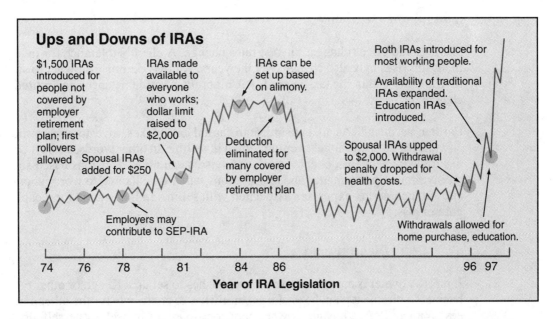

Ups and Downs of IRAs

$1,500 IRAs introduced for people not covered by employer retirement plan; first rollovers allowed

Spousal IRAs added for $250

Employers may contribute to SEP-IRA

IRAs made available to everyone who works; dollar limit raised to $2,000

IRAs can be set up based on alimony.

Deduction eliminated for many covered by employer retirement plan

Spousal IRAs upped to $2,000. Withdrawal penalty dropped for health costs.

Roth IRAs introduced for most working people.

Availability of traditional IRAs expanded. Education IRAs introduced.

Withdrawals allowed for home purchase, education.

74   76   78   81   84   86   96   97

Year of IRA Legislation

1974: IRAs were first introduced in 1974, as part of comprehensive national pension reform that was ushered in by the Employee Retirement Income Security Act of 1974 (ERISA). The first IRAs were offered as an alternative for individuals who were not covered by an employer-sponsored retirement plan and the original annual contribution limit was $1,500. Over the years, a series of changes opened IRAs to more and more people.

1976: The first change came in 1976 when nonworking spouses were first allowed to open IRA, albeit with the low annual contribution limit of $250. In 1978, a mechanism was created that allowed employers to set up and maintain a program of IRAs for employees called a Simplified Employee Pension (SEP).

1981: The big change in IRAs came with the Economic Recovery Tax Act of 1981 (ERTA), which greatly expanded the availability of IRAs to any working individual, regardless of participation in an employer-sponsored plan. At the same time, the annual contribution limit was increased to $2,000.

1984: Alimony recipients became entitled to establish IRAs based on any taxable alimony they received.

1986: The Tax Reform Act of 1986 drastically altered IRA rules by partially resurrecting the concept that made IRAs available only to those who did not participate in an employer-sponsored retirement plan. Under the new rules, participating employees with incomes over fairly modest thresholds could still contribute to an IRA but could not take a deduction on their income tax return.

1996: The 1986 legislation significantly restricted the value of IRAs as a financial tool for many Americans, and the situation remained unchanged for ten years. But then the tide began to turn. In 1996, tax legislation gave the first-ever increase in the contribution limit for IRAs set up for nonworking spouses. The limit was increased from $250 to $2,000, equal to the limit for the working spouse. Also in 1996, restrictions on IRA withdrawals before age 59½ were eased, and the early-withdrawal penalty was dropped on withdrawals used for certain health expenses.

1997: The Taxpayer Relief Act of 1997 promises to be the biggest shot in the arm for IRAs since ERTA expanded their availability in 1981. The income thresholds for deductible IRAs were increased and two new types of IRAs were introduced—the Roth IRA, which promises to be very popular, and the education IRA. In addition, two new types of preretirement withdrawals were introduced—for education and for first-home purchase expenses.

but it does not insist on any annual deposit. (However, you should be aware that certain investments or custodians may require certain minimum deposits even though the IRS does not.)

Investment Flexibility

Markets and prices change. Interest rates change. A client's tolerance for investment surprises may also change over the years. An IRA permits its owner to switch investments within the tax-favored IRA umbrella as circumstances and attitudes change.

Further, because IRAs are not subject to capital gains taxes, investors enjoy the tax advantages of institutional over individual investing. In other words, when it comes to selling investments, clients and their advisors can make decisions based solely on investment performance and expectations rather than having to worry about the current income-tax exposures associated with selling an investment for a capital gain or loss.

IRAs Can "Discriminate"

If an IRA owner is a business owner who wishes to set up a Keogh or other type of business retirement plan, he or she generally has to contribute for the other employees. With an IRA, a business owner may contribute for himself or herself alone.

A business owner who desires the simplicity of recordkeeping with an IRA, as opposed to a Keogh or other type of "qualified plan," may establish a simplified employee pension (SEP) program and under this plan, fund IRAs for employees as well as for himself or herself.

IRAs Have a Place Before Retirement

IRAs are designed primarily to help investors save for retirement, so withdrawals before the age of 59½ may be subject to an early withdrawal penalty. But not always! Many types of withdrawals—for education, first-time home purchases, an early-retirement annuity, disability and so on—may qualify to be taken free of penalty (and in the case of a Roth IRA, often free of tax). With money in their IRAs, your clients will be better prepared for life before retirement than if they let this investment opportunity pass them by.

Great Flexibility After Age 59½

IRAs provide their owners with great flexibility to adapt to changes in their particular financial and employment circumstances during the important years between 59½ and 70½ (i.e., the years during which IRA funds may be withdrawn without penalty and before they are required to be withdrawn from traditional IRAs). This period of maximum flexibility is increased with a Roth IRA, because there are no required distributions during the investor's lifetime. If your clients over age 59½ are still earning compensation, they may continue to make IRA contributions during those years, even though they are also making withdrawals.

Income for a Lifetime

If IRAs are used to provide retirement income, their payout can be designed to produce an income stream that the IRA owner cannot outlive. This is accomplished by *annuitizing* the distributions, which will be discussed in more detail in Chapter 4.

IRAs Can Be Inherited by Anyone

An IRA can be inherited by one or more people in the event that the owner dies before the money in the account is fully distributed. If an individual chooses to name his or her spouse as the beneficiary and the IRA owner dies before distributions from his or her IRA start, then the spouse may delay taking distributions—and paying the tax—until the year when the original account owner would have reached 70½. Otherwise, the spouse may choose to roll over the account to his or her own IRA.

■ ROTH OR TRADITIONAL IRAs?

The big question for your clients will be whether to invest in a traditional IRA or a Roth IRA. This question and the answer to it lies behind much of the rest of this course. Before we go into the details, however, let's take a moment to look at the big picture.

The difference between a Roth and a traditional IRA involves the treatment of contributions, on the front end, and withdrawals, on the back end. A traditional IRA offers the *potential* of deductible contributions, and if contributions were deducted, withdrawals will be fully taxable. You'll learn more about these rules in Chapter 2.

Roth IRA contributions, on the other hand, are totally nondeductible. Tax benefits are "backloaded," which means that qualifying withdrawals are totally tax free. So the choice is between a deduction now (the traditional IRA) and tax-free withdrawals sometime in the future (the Roth IRA). You learn more about these rules in Chapter 3.

In helping your clients to choose between these two types of IRA, you will first have to determine which type they are eligible for. Many people are eligible for both, but others are eligible for only one.

- Eligibility to open a Roth IRA is phased out for joint tax filers with incomes between $150,000 and $160,000. Clients with income above these levels may not contribute to a Roth. For single taxpayers, the phaseout range is $95,000 to $110,000.

- Anyone with earned income can contribute to a traditional IRA, but the right to deduct contributions is phased out for single individuals who are covered by their employer's retirement plan and whose income is between $30,000 and $40,000 in 1998 (between $50,000 and $60,000 for married individuals who file joint tax returns). Above this, no deduction is permitted. Clients who are ineligible for the deduction, but are eligible for a Roth IRA, would be best advised to contribute to a Roth IRA.

- Nonworking spouses are eligible to open either type of IRA (regardless of whether the working spouse is covered by an employer's plan) if the couple files jointly. This right is phased out for incomes between $150,000 and $160,000. Above this level, a nonworking spouse is left to making nondeductible contributions to a traditional IRA.

If your client is eligible to open only one type of IRA, your analysis is over. There's no choice. But if your client is eligible for both types, you'll have to ask two questions:

1. Which is more valuable—a deduction now (that you get with a traditional IRA) or tax-free withdrawals later (that you get with a Roth IRA)?

2. Will your client bank the tax savings that comes from deducting a contribution to a traditional IRA?

Let's take the second question first. The fact of the matter is that, everything being equal, a qualifying withdrawal from a Roth IRA will always be larger. Why? Because there is no tax on a qualifying withdrawal from the Roth. Withdrawals from traditional IRAs are subject to tax.

But stopping there means you are forgetting the value of the tax deduction your client could get by contributing to a traditional IRA. This value doesn't show up in the IRA account itself. The question is whether your client can capture the value of the tax deduction—say, by investing the tax savings. If so, you have a basis for answering the first question.

Another way of asking the first question is this: If your client invests the tax savings, will that savings *plus* the traditional IRA be more valuable than a Roth IRA? The short answer is that, if your client expects to be in a lower tax bracket at retirement, the traditional IRA would be better. Otherwise, based on tax considerations alone, choose the Roth.

If it sounds like a lot of "ifs" go into choosing a traditional IRA, you're right. Many people will focus on the amount that will be available to them at retirement from the IRA account itself and choose a Roth. Many will look at preretirement availability of funds and choose a Roth again (see Chapter 4 for a comparison of preretirement withdrawals from both types of IRAs).

Roth IRAs are very attractive, but in the right circumstances, the choice of a Roth is far from automatic.

■ IRAs—MANY VARIATIONS ON A THEME

Most Americans are familiar with how the basic IRA works: a person independently deposits money, up to $2,000 annually, into a retirement account that's offered by a financial institution, such as a bank or mutual fund. This applies to the traditional IRA as well as to the Roth IRA. Yet, there are several other types of IRA arrangements with which many Americans (and even some financial representatives) may be less familiar.

This section will begin by exploring various types of IRAs, including regular IRAs, IRA annuities, IRAs established by businesses and other entities (rather than by individuals), as well as spousal and inherited IRAs.

In addition, we'll compare different IRA investment providers including banks, which typically offer certificates of deposit (CDs); brokerage houses, which offer a wide range of securities and mutual funds; and life insurance companies, which offer both fixed and variable annuities.

By definition, an individual retirement account is a *trust* or *custodial account* set up in the United States for the exclusive benefit of an individual taxpayer and his or her beneficiaries. According to the IRS, the account is actually created by means of a written IRA document. The IRS requires this document to demonstrate that the IRA satisfies all of the following requirements:

- The account must have a trustee or custodian. This custodian must be a bank, a federally insured credit union, a savings and loan association or an entity approved by the IRS to serve as a trustee or custodian (insurance and securities companies generally fall into this category).

- The trustee or custodian generally cannot accept contributions greater than $2,000 per individual account, per year. However, rollover contributions and employer contributions to simplified employee pensions (SEPs) can be more than $2,000.

- Contributions that do not involve rollovers must be cash, checks or money orders.

- The investor must be fully vested in the amount in his or her IRA. This means that the account owner has a nonforfeitable right to the total assets in his or her account at all times.

- Money in the investor's account cannot be used to buy a life insurance policy.

- Assets in an IRA cannot be combined with other personal assets.

- The owner of a traditional IRA must begin receiving at least partial distributions from his or her account no later than April 1 of the year following the year when he or she turns 70½. This rule does *not* apply to a Roth IRA.

With these seven requirements for an IRA in mind, let's look at the other types of IRAs available.

Individual Retirement Annuities

An *individual retirement annuity* is established by purchasing an annuity contract or an endowment contract from a life insurance company in compliance with certain standards and guidelines.

Annuities are purchased through the payment of premiums to an insurance company. Only the annuity owner and the beneficiaries who survive that owner may receive payments from the annuity. The IRS has a list of individual retirement annuity requirements:

- The owner's entire interest in the annuity account must be nonforfeitable.

- The owner may not transfer any portion of the annuity to any party other than the issuer (e.g., the life insurance company).

- Annuity contracts issued after November 6, 1978, must provide for flexible payment of premiums. The thought behind this requirement is that if an owner's compensation changes from year to year, contributions to the individual retirement annuity must also be able to change accordingly.

- The owner cannot contribute more than $2,000 per year to his or her individual retirement annuity. In addition, any refunded premiums must be used to pay for future premiums or to buy more benefits before the end of the calendar year when the owner receives the refund. This requirement minimizes the potential for "accidental" premature distributions.

Many investors in regular (nonannuity) IRAs may direct the IRA custodian to purchase an annuity contract when it comes time to retire (as discussed in Chapter 4). Alternatively, investors who use regular IRAs before retirement, while they build up their savings, may convert ("roll over") to an individual retirement *annuity* when they are ready to start making withdrawals.

Regardless of the method used, the value of the annuity after retirement is the same. Regular IRAs are like any other form of savings: when the money runs out, the money runs out. And many retirees could outlive their retirement savings without an annuity. This is not possible with the annuity form of IRA because the issuing insurance company can provide a guarantee that payments will continue for life.

Rollover IRAs

An IRA *rollover* normally involves a tax-free distribution of cash or other assets from one retirement program to another. Rollover contributions to IRAs may come from other IRAs or from qualified retirement plans established by the IRA owner's employer or former employer.

A special type of rollover—from a traditional IRA to a Roth IRA—is not a tax-free transaction, but is treated as a rollover because it is subject to many of the same rules.

Rollover accounts are *not* subject to the $2,000 annual contribution limits that are associated with regular IRAs. We will examine IRA rollovers and transfers in greater detail in Chapter 4.

Employer and Employee Association Trust Accounts

An employer, labor union or other employee association may establish a trust to provide IRAs for its employees or members. The rules for IRAs also apply to employer and employee association trust accounts.

Simplified Pensions

A *simplified employee pension* (SEP) is a written arrangement that permits certain employers to make deductible contributions to an employee's IRA, which is generally referred to as a SEP-IRA. A *savings incentive match plans for employees* (SIMPLE) is another employer arrangement that uses IRAs to provide retirement benefits for employees. SEPs and SIMPLEs will be discussed at greater length in Chapter 6.

Spousal IRAs

An IRA owner may be able to establish and contribute to an IRA for his or her spouse, regardless of whether the spouse received compensation in the taxable year. This arrangement is known as a *spousal IRA*.

However, an individual cannot set up an IRA that is co-owned with the spouse. The IRA owner and spouse must maintain *separate* IRAs. An individual who has already established an IRA who later wishes to set one up for his or her spouse may keep the existing IRA and start another one for the spouse.

To contribute to a spousal IRA, several requirements must be met:

- The IRA owner and spouse must be married at the end of the tax year for which the spousal contribution is being made.

- The IRA owner and spouse must file a joint tax return (married, filing jointly) for the tax year that corresponds to the spousal contribution.

- In the case of a traditional IRA, the spouse on whose behalf the contribution is being made must be under age 70½ at the end of the tax year when the spousal contribution applies.

- The contributing spouse must have taxable compensation for the applicable year, while the noncontributing spouse must either have no compensation or if eligible compensation is less than $2,000, choose to be treated as having no compensation for the tax year.

Inherited IRAs

IRAs can be inherited just like any other property. Beneficiaries, however, must observe special rules.

Nonspousal beneficiaries may not make contributions (including rollover contributions) to the inherited IRA, nor may they roll the account over into another type of noninherited account. However, nonspousal beneficiaries still enjoy the same tax deferrals as do other IRA owners. There is no federal income tax liability on the assets in the IRA until the beneficiary actually receives distributions from it.

Spousal beneficiaries have more options. A beneficiary who is a surviving spouse may elect to treat an inherited IRA as his or her own. Thus, he or she can make contributions, including rollover contributions, to the inherited IRA.

■ IRA INVESTMENT PROVIDERS

IRAs can be established with several types of institutions. Most banks, savings and loan associations, mutual funds, stock brokerage firms and insurance companies offer IRAs that satisfy the Internal Revenue Code's various requirements. How does a consumer decide what type of institution to turn to when setting up an IRA?

The choice of institution will be based, in part, on an individual's investment preference for funding the IRA. It will depend on the individual's age, time till retirement, tolerance for risk and other factors. Banks, brokerage houses and insurance companies all have their place.

Banks

Banks may limit their investment alternatives for IRA accounts to fixed-rate and variable-rate CDs, passbook accounts and money-market deposit accounts. These investments are protected by FDIC insurance, up to $100,000 per person, per bank. The fees, if any, charged for opening and maintaining an IRA are relatively small.

Commercial banks may also market and manage common funds for IRA customers, giving them a wider range of investment choices and flexibility. They may also provide other conveniences, such as transfers from checking accounts and direct payroll deductions.

Today you may find securities representatives operating within the premises of their banks. Because of prohibitions against banks operating as securities brokerages, securities desks within banks often represent an entity separate from the bank.

Brokerage Houses

Through "self-directed" IRAs, brokerage houses offer the widest range of investment alternatives. Some offer everything from money-market funds and stocks and bonds to limited partnership interests in real estate and other endeavors.

ILL. 1.2 ■ *Investment Choices When Interest Rates Are Low*

IRA contributions should not be delayed in anticipation of higher interest rates. However, investment choices should be made with potential higher interest rate opportunities in mind. The earlier an IRA contribution is made, the sooner earnings on the contribution begin to accrue on a tax-deferred basis. In turn, this leads to a greater compounding of interest which, over the life of the IRA, can mean thousands of extra dollars.

Investors who anticipate a rise in interest rates may consider nonfixed investments for the short run, such as money-market funds or market deposit accounts. When interest rates increase, the money can be switched to a higher-yielding fixed vehicle such as a certificate of deposit.

Fees to open and maintain IRAs in brokerage houses are generally higher than with other IRA providers. Some may charge a fee based on the number of separate investments held within the account, while others may charge a fee that relates to the dollar value of the account. To attract larger IRA rollover business, some brokerages waive or reduce fees for accounts over a certain amount.

Some brokerage houses suggest that a different IRA investment be selected each year to foster investment diversification and thus provide the relative safety and stability that's generally associated with diversification. As long as the self-directed IRA owner maintains the same brokerage house as custodian, he or she may move IRA assets among different investments to enhance diversification or to pursue the best return. This offers a significant advantage over investing in bank certificates where an investor may be unable to dispose of the investment without facing interest penalties.

Brokerage-provided, self-directed IRA accounts do *not* offer the guaranteed return or safety that accompanies bank deposits, but if the account is invested in U.S. government securities, it does enjoy the "full faith and credit" of the federal government.

IRA owners have numerous options available to them when it comes to investing their savings through brokerage houses. From stocks and bonds to mutual funds, IRA owners can make investment choices depending on their current needs and long-term goals.

Stocks

Stocks are units of ownership in corporations that have historically provided a much better hedge against inflation than debt securities, such as bonds.

Zero-Coupon Bonds

Zero-coupon bonds may appeal to investors in IRAs and other tax-deferred retirement accounts because they virtually eliminate the problem of reinvesting interest payments at lower rates of return if interest rates fall (assuming that the bonds are held to maturity).

A zero-coupon bond derives its name from the simple fact that the bond is issued with a 0 percent coupon rate. The return on a zero-coupon bond comes from the gradual increase in the bond's price from the discount to face value, which it reaches at maturity. Investors should be aware that any zero-coupon bond's absence of current income makes it more volatile than interest-bearing bonds.

Certain zero-coupon bonds are based on underlying U.S. Treasury issues. They are often marketed by brokerage houses under names associated with animals. Examples include CATs (certificates of accrual on Treasury securities) or COUGARS (certificates on government receipts). An investor who is buying one of these is not really buying the Treasury security itself. Rather, the investor acquires a receipt entitling him or her to the value of a Treasury security held in escrow.

The government directly issues zero-coupon Treasuries through its securities called STRIPS (separate trading of registered interest and principal of securities). Because they have direct government backing and avoid complicated trust arrangements, STRIPS yield a little less interest than other government-backed zero securities.

Mutual Funds

Mutual funds are popular choices for IRA accounts, because they offer a wide range of investment alternatives. There are families of mutual funds ranging from conservative to very aggressive growth and enhanced yield funds. The IRA investor may move from one fund to another without tax or transfer consequences, as long as the move is within the same fund family and involves the same custodian or trustee. Typically, investors in a family of funds can transfer assets (usually for a minimal fee) with just a phone call or by filling out a few forms.

Minimum contributions to set up an IRA through most mutual funds range from $25 to $500, while subsequent contributions to add to an IRA are usually for smaller amounts. Some funds also arrange to have withdrawals made automatically from your clients' checking accounts and placed into your clients' IRAs.

A major advantage of mutual funds is that they offer significant diversification for a small investment. If an IRA owner invests $2,000 in a common stock fund, then he or she can typically buy a piece of 80 or 90 companies.

The fund's prospectus. Every mutual fund states its financial objective clearly in its prospectus. Before your client may invest in a mutual fund, he or she must be presented with a copy of the fund's prospectus.

Although the prospectus may be intimidating reading material, the IRA owner should be encouraged to read it. The prospectus provides the IRA owner with the necessary information to understand the mutual fund's objectives. The IRA owner can then decide whether the fund's investment goals are compatible with his or her own financial goals.

For example, suppose you have a client who is nearing retirement and who will depend on the IRA as the major source of retirement income. This client may wish to avoid mutual funds that emphasize speculative investments that pay little or no dividends and may not enjoy capital gains for years.

A prospectus also reveals the specific investments in the fund's portfolio. It should also disclose all fees charged by the fund.

Types of mutual funds. There are many different types of mutual funds that your client can select. The most popular are:

- **Diversified common stock funds**. These funds invest in a wide variety of common stocks in many different industries. Their emphasis can range from moderate income with moderate capital growth and relatively good stability of principal ("blue-chip funds") to minimal income with maximum capital growth and little stability of principal ("aggressive growth funds"). Aggressive growth funds typically invest in relatively small companies that are in growing industries.

- **Bond funds**. These funds invest in debt instruments with initial maturities exceeding one year. Bond funds may further describe themselves as investing primarily in either corporate debt securities or in U.S. government and agency securities.

- **Money-market funds**. Money-market funds invest in short-term debt instruments, such as Treasury bills, negotiable certificates of deposit, bankers acceptances, commercial paper and Eurodollars. Money-market funds, except in periods of high inflation, have provided relatively modest returns, perhaps in exchange for very high liquidity.

- **Asset allocation funds**. These funds invest in stocks, bonds, money-market instruments and other investments such as precious metals and real estate. Allocation among the categories is determined by the fund's managers who may try to time allocations based on interest rates and their predictions of movements in the stock market.

- **Index funds**. These funds attempt to duplicate the performance of a commonly followed stock market indicator such as Standard & Poor's 500 Index or the NYSE Composite Index. The objective is to create a portfolio that has the same securities in the same proportions as the index. Index funds reflect the belief that outperforming the market on a risk-adjusted basis is virtually impossible.

- **Sector funds**. These funds invest primarily in the common stock of a single industry. These include financial services, gold-oriented, health/biotechnology, real estate, science and technology, and utility industries. Although diversified among various companies within one industry, the lack of diversification among industries makes sector funds riskier than more diversified funds.

Insurance Companies

The insurance industry's basic IRA product is the flexible premium annuity, which may be either fixed or variable. With a fixed annuity, your clients are guaranteed a maximum rate of return for the first one to five years and then a minimum rate of return thereafter. Typically, the written minimum guaranteed return over a long-term period is low.

Fixed IRA annuities provide safety and stability and reasonable rates of return relative to their risk. However, returns may be lower than those of other investments. Although fixed annuities are vulnerable to inflation, retirement income from an insurance annuity does have the advantage of being guaranteed. Your clients do not have to worry over loss of retirement income because of the ups and downs of the economy.

With variable annuities, your client is given a choice of several different investment portfolios. Just as with a family of mutual funds, your client can switch from one fund to another without a rollover or transfer. Usually, an insurance company group will include one or more common stock funds, a money-market fund and a bond or fixed-income fund.

Expense charges and fees vary greatly among insurance companies offering IRA annuities. Today most annuity companies have adopted "backload" charges that will be assessed if your clients withdraw their money before a specific time period has elapsed, usually from 7 to 10 years. These "withdrawal charges" decline each year the annuity contract is held until they eventually disappear.

Collectibles

The Internal Revenue Code penalizes an IRA owner who directs his or her investments into collectibles. Examples of collectibles include artwork, rugs, antiques, metals, gems, stamps, rare books, coins and any other tangible personal property characterized as such by the IRS. The Internal Revenue Code provides that if any IRA assets are used to acquire a collectible, the amount is treated as a distribution, which is therefore taxable to the owner.

However, IRAs are permitted to invest in certain U.S. Treasury-minted gold and silver coins, including one-ounce, half-ounce, quarter-ounce and tenth-of-an-ounce gold bullion coins and a one-ounce silver bullion coin. Coins issued by states are also permissible IRA investments. Beginning in 1998, restrictions on this type of investment were liberalized to allow investment in platinum coins and any gold, silver, platinum or palladium bullion of a type that is traded in the futures market.

■ CHAPTER 1 QUESTIONS FOR REVIEW

1. Which of the statements below best describes the impact of the Taxpayer Relief Act of 1997 (TRA '97) on IRAs?

   A. Few investors could make IRA contributions.

   B. More investors could benefit by making IRA contributions.

   C. Contribution limits would be adjusted to account for annual inflation.

   D. All working Americans could deduct annual IRA contributions.

2. All of the following are advantages of IRA ownership EXCEPT

   A. tax-deferred compounding

   B. unlimited annual contributions

   C. investment flexibility

   D. the right to name a beneficiary

3. Which of the following is true of BOTH a traditional and a Roth IRA?

   A. Contributions may be deductible.

   B. Withdrawals from IRAs held for five years are tax free.

   C. No tax is due on earnings as long as investments are held in the IRA.

   D. A 10 percent penalty applies to all withdrawals before age 59½.

4. Assuming that it is not a rollover, which of the following may be accepted by an IRA custodian?

   A. $1,000 worth of Treasury bonds

   B. $2,000 in cash

   C. $3,000 in cash

   D. $5,000 worth of readily traded stocks

5. Hal and May Wilson, a married couple, file their income taxes jointly. Because May does not work outside the home, Hal plans to establish and fund an IRA for his wife. This arrangement is best described as a

   A. joint IRA

   B. joint and last survivor IRA

   C. spousal IRA

   D. marital deduction IRA

2

Traditional IRAs: Contributions and Deductions

T here have been so many changes in IRA rules that it is important to say that the traditional IRA, which people have depended on for more than 20 years, still exists and is still an important vehicle for tax-deferred retirement savings. The newcomer Roth IRA supplements the traditional IRA but does not replace it. Some of your clients will do better with a Roth IRA and some will do better with a traditional IRA. And many will end up owning both types.

This chapter takes a close look at the rules governing traditional IRA contributions and deductions. We'll cover Roth IRAs in the next chapter. Many of the rules are the same for both. Since many people are familiar with traditional IRAs, the differences will be highlighted in Chapter 3. Included in this chapter are the limits on contributions to traditional IRAs and the question of when an income tax deduction is allowed for those contributions.

Being able to deduct contributions is one of the great incentives for setting up a traditional IRA. It is important to stress, however, that *nondeductible* contributions may be made to a traditional IRA. This is still true, even though nondeductible contributions made to a Roth IRA yield even greater tax benefit. As you will see, however, some people won't qualify either for a Roth IRA or for a deductible traditional IRA—but they can still open a nondeductible IRA.

Consequently, the rules governing the size and timing of contributions are separate from those governing the tax deductibility. We will cover the contribution rules first and then move on to the tax issue.

■ ■ ■ ■ ■

■ CONTRIBUTIONS TO TRADITIONAL IRAs

As soon as a traditional IRA is set up, the IRA investor may make contributions to the account through its custodian, trustee or other administrator. Contributions must be in the form of money: only cash, checks or money orders will be accepted by IRA custodians. An individual may not contribute property, including investments, to a regular IRA. (Although the law allows rollover IRAs to accept property as well as cash, many IRA plan documents don't accept any contribution in the form of property.)

Individuals may contribute to their IRAs each year that they qualify. Even if an IRA investor doesn't qualify to make contributions for the current year, the amounts contributed for past years in which he or she did qualify can, of course, remain in the IRA.

To "qualify" the IRA investor must have received "taxable compensation" as defined in the Internal Revenue Code. Typically, this is what your clients earn from working—that is, their yearly compensation. The rule regarding taxable compensation applies regardless of whether the contribution is deductible.

What Is Compensation?

For purposes of determining IRA eligibility, the IRS defines *compensation* as:

- wages;

- salaries;

- tips;

- professional fees;

- bonuses;

- commissions; and

- other amounts received for providing personal services.

If an IRA investor is employed, compensation is normally the amount shown in Box 1 of his or her W-2 form furnished by the employer.

Self-Employment Income

If the IRA investor is self-employed—as a sole proprietor or as a partner in a partnership—compensation is considered the net earnings from his or her trade or business if the services materially contribute to the income of the business. (Income earned as a silent partner is *not* considered compensation for this purpose. If an IRA owner invests in a partnership but does not provide services that are a material income-producing factor to the partnership, his or her share of partnership income will not be treated as compensation for IRA purposes.)

Today, more and more individuals hold jobs with companies as well as operate their own small businesses. When individuals have both self-employment income and salaries and wages, the IRS will consider compensation to be the total of those amounts. Sometimes, however, a business owner may have a net loss from operating his or her own businesses. When this occurs, the loss should *not* be subtracted from salaries or wages received when calculating total compensation for IRA purposes.

ILL. 2.1 ■ *What Income May Not Be Used for an IRA?*

For IRA purposes, the following is *not* considered compensation by the IRS:

- earnings from property, such as rental income, interest income and dividend income;
- pension and annuity income;
- any deferred compensation received (compensation amounts postponed from a past year);
- foreign-earned income and housing cost amounts that are excluded from taxable income; and
- any other amounts that are excluded from taxable income.

Alimony and Separate Maintenance

All taxable alimony and separate maintenance income that an individual receives under a divorce or separate maintenance decree is treated as compensation. If an individual receives taxable alimony but does not work, it's still possible for him or her to make an eligible IRA contribution on the basis of alimony received.

Contribution Limits

The most that an individual can contribute for any single year to an IRA is the lesser of:

- 100 percent of the IRA owner's compensation that was included for federal income tax reporting; or

- $2,000.

This yearly contribution limit does *not* change when an individual maintains more than one IRA, nor is the limit influenced by whether the contribution is deductible. The yearly contribution limit is an umbrella limit. It applies to both traditional and Roth IRAs. An investor may divide the contribution between the two types or between as many accounts as he or she wishes, but the total contributed may not exceed $2,000, or 100 percent of compensation.

If your clients fail to use their entire limit, they may not contribute more in a later year to make up the difference. Unfortunately, the IRS does not allow retroactive or cumulative IRA contributions.

Also, brokerage commissions that individuals pay in conjunction with their IRAs do not increase the annual contribution limit nor are they deductible.

Trustee or custodian administrative and reporting fees that are billed to an IRA owner are *not* subject to the contribution limit. To avoid confusion, however, your clients may wish to use a separate check for their annual IRA contribution and another for their annual IRA maintenance fee. Under certain circumstances, the tax-payer may be able to deduct these fees as a miscellaneous deduction.

Married Couples and Contribution Limits

If a husband and wife both work and each earn at least $2,000 during the year, they may each contribute up to full $2,000 limit on the strength of their own compensation. The money must be placed in separate accounts, as there is no such thing as a joint IRA.

If only one spouse earns over $2,000, the couple may still contribute the full $2,000 *each* to separate IRAs, provided that the couple files a joint tax return and the couple's joint compensation exceeds $4,000. If the couple's joint compensation is less than $4,000, their contribution limit is the amount of their joint compensation—and this may be divided between them any way they wish.

This is a big change from the rule that was in place before 1997. Before that time, a one-income married couple was limited to a $2,250 contribution. Now both spouses may set up IRAs and take advantage of the full $2,000 contribution limit regardless of how many breadwinners there are. Your clients may have gotten into the habit of ignoring the spousal IRA because of the low $250 extra limit, but now it pays to take advantage of the opportunity.

Spouses have benefited in another way by recent changes. Before 1998, your client could have the IRA contribution *deduction* curtailed if her husband (or his wife) was covered by his (or her) employer-sponsored retirement plan. As you will see, when we get to the discussion of deductions, spouses' deductions are no longer subject to this restriction.

This is a significant difference for one-income married couples where the earning spouse is covered by an employer-sponsored retirement plan. Under the old rules, this couple might have been limited to a $2,250 contribution with zero deduction. Now, this same couple may contribute $4,000 and deduct half that amount.

When to Contribute

Individuals can make contributions to their own IRAs (or to spousal IRAs) for a given year any time during that year or by the due date for filing a tax return for that year. Extensions to filing a tax return do *not* extend the IRA contribution deadline.

IRA investors may file their tax returns showing one or more IRA contributions before they actually make the contribution. The contribution must, however, be made by the due date of the return, usually April 15 of the year following the tax year for which the return is being filed.

Individuals who open or contribute to an IRA must make sure that their custodian or trustee credits the contribution to the correct year. Mistakes are most likely to happen when contributions are made between January 1 and April 15. During this period, IRA contributions could apply either to the past tax year or to the current one.

Sponsors (custodians, trustees, etc.) are required to report the year for which an IRA owner's contributions apply. Sponsors that fail to do so can be fined $50 for each reporting failure.

When individuals have several IRAs or make a number of small contributions for each tax year rather than a single large contribution, it's easy to make an excess contribution simply by losing track of the number and amount of prior contributions for a given tax year. Therefore, IRA owners need to carefully record their contributions for a given year so such mistakes won't occur.

IRA contributions may be made any time during the year. In fact, IRA owners can wait until April 15 to make their IRA contributions for the previous year. For example, Joe may make an IRA contribution on April 15, 1999, and apply it—and any deduction he may take—to his 1998 income tax return. However, the earlier an individual invests in his or her IRA each year, the faster the IRA account will grow. Following this simple strategy can put the IRA owner thousands of dollars ahead at retirement time.

Of course, it's not always possible for your clients to make their entire IRA contributions in early January when most are saddled with holiday bills. Nevertheless, to make the most of their IRAs, encourage your clients to bunch their contributions close to the start of each year rather than waiting until the April 15 tax deadline of the following year. By investing early, your clients' contributions will be compounding tax sheltered for an extra 15½ months.

ILL. 2.2 ■ *Should You Contribute Early to an IRA?*

IRAs are just like other investments programs: the earlier investors begin saving, the more money they will have to spend when they've reached their goal.

Let's take Charlie and Monica as an example. They each decided to open an IRA in 1998. Charlie opened his on the earliest possible date: January 1, 1998. Monica waited until the due date for her 1998 tax return: April 15, 1999. Charlie consistently contributed on the first day of the year and Monica consistently contributed on tax day of the following year.

Twenty years later, compare the value of Charlie's and Monica's IRAs (assuming that they each earned 10 percent on their investments). On December 31, 2018, Charlie's account will be worth $140,805. Monica's account will be worth $122,710. Charlie will be ahead by $18,095 by investing early.

Of course, when a client comes to open an IRA on April 15, you can't go back and undo the "damage." What your client can do, though, is double up the contribution, earmarking $2,000 for the previous year and $2,000 for the current year.

If Monica doubled up on her contribution on April 15, 1999, and continued with April 15 contributions of $2,000 each year, her account will be worth $135,813 at the end of 2018. Shifting to a January 1 contribution would increase the value of the account to $138,756.

■ DEDUCTIBILITY OF IRA CONTRIBUTIONS

We've noted that there's a big difference between IRA contribution limits and deduction limits. Your client may be eligible to deduct the full maximum contribution of $2,000. Or he or she may be ineligible for the deduction because he or she participates in an employer-sponsored retirement plan. It all depends on your client's income level. The cutoff levels are fairly low but increase every year, as you will see. The two points to look for, then, are participation in an employer-sponsored plan and income level.

Before moving on to the question of whether your client is considered a participant in an employer-sponsored plan, let's consider the importance of the deduction question. The deduction is one of the prime reasons an individual would choose a traditional IRA rather than a Roth IRA.

In making the choice between the two types of IRA, then, the critical question is whether your client is covered by an employer plan.

Participants in an Employer's Retirement Plan

The law places deduction restrictions on your client if he or she is an *active participant* in the employer's plan. We use this term here interchangeably with the term *covered*. The purpose of the term is to indicate that the mere fact that your client's employer has a retirement plan is not enough. Your client must be deriving some actual or potential economic benefit by being "covered" by the plan.

Every year employers send their workers the Form W-2 Wage and Tax Statement for income-tax reporting purposes. The statement includes a box that indicates whether the employee is covered by the employer's plan for the year. The form should have a mark in the "Pension Plan" box if the employee is, indeed, a participant in the plan.

If, after looking at their W-2, your clients are still not certain whether they are covered by their employers' retirement plans, they should then ask their employers. An employer's human resources or employee benefits department should have this information readily available.

Employer Plans

What is an employer-sponsored retirement plan? It is a retirement plan an employer sets up for the benefit of its employees and their beneficiaries. For purposes of the IRA deduction rules, an employer retirement plan is considered to be a:

- **Qualified pension plan**. This can be a profit-sharing, stock bonus or money-purchase plan that complies with Internal Revenue Code requirements. (Keogh plans are also included in this definition.)

- **401(k) plan**. This is an arrangement in a profit-sharing or stock bonus plan that allows an eligible employee to choose to take part of his or her compensation from an employer in cash or have the employer pay it into the 401(k) plan.

- **Union plan**. This is a qualified stock bonus, pension or profit-sharing plan created by a collective bargaining agreement between employee representatives and one or more employers.

- **Qualified annuity plan**. This type of plan allows employees to fund their annuities through salary reductions. These contributions are made with pretax dollars, thus lowering the employees' current taxable income.

- **Federal, state or local government plan**. This type of plan is established by some political entity or agency for its employees. (Certain state-operated deferred compensation plans, known as Section 457 plans, are *not* included in this definition.)

- **Tax-sheltered annuity plan**. This plan is established for employees of public schools, hospitals and certain other tax-exempt organizations.

- **Simplified plans**. There are two types of simplified plans that are treated as employer plans: Simplified Employee Pensions (SEPs) and Savings Incentive Match PLans for Employees (SIMPLEs).

- **501(c)(18) trust**. This is a certain type of tax-exempt trust created before June 25, 1959, that is funded only by employee contributions.

Although there are many varieties of employer plans, they fall into two broad categories: defined-contribution plans and defined-benefit plans. If your client's employer fails to satisfy the question of whether your client is an active participant in the plan (either directly or on the client's W-2), you can analyze the plans as follows.

Defined-Contribution Plan

A *defined-contribution plan* provides a separate account for each person covered under the plan. Ultimately, benefits will depend on amounts contributed or allocated to each account and their corresponding tax-deferred earnings. Types of defined contribution plans include profit-sharing plans, stock bonus plans and money-purchase (pension) plans.

An employee is considered to be a participant in a defined contribution plan when his or her employer makes a contribution for the plan year or any forfeiture is allocated to his or her account.

Simplified plans and 401(k) plans are defined-contribution plans, and contributions made by your client to these types of plans are considered to be "employer contributions." If your client contributes to one of these types of plans, he or she is an active participant and subject to the deduction restrictions that apply to his or her income level.

Defined-Benefit Plan

Simply put, a *defined-benefit plan* is any plan that is *not* a defined-contribution plan. Contributions to a defined-benefit plan are based on a calculation of the amount of contributions necessary to provide definite benefits to plan participants.

ILL. 2.3 ■ *Who Is Covered When Your Client Is Married?*

Tina and Richard Lucas are married. Tina works for Empire Foundry, Inc. and is a participant in its 401(k) plan. Richard works for Inventors, Ltd., a company that has no retirement plan.

Richard earns a generous income from his work and, since he is not covered by an employer-sponsored plan, may deduct a full $2,000 contribution to a traditional IRA. His ability to deduct IRA contributions is unaffected by Tina's participation in her employer's plan.

Tina, on the other hand, may have her IRA deduction limited. It all depends on her income. The dollar limits change every year.

If your clients meet the minimum age (usually 21) and service requirements (usually one year of service with the employer) to participate in a defined-benefit plan for the plan year that ends with their tax years, they will be considered covered under the plan. "Active participant" status will apply even if your client declines to be covered under the plan or did not perform the minimum number of hours of work to accrue a benefit for the year.

Even if a participant is not vested in the amount allocated to his or her defined-contribution plan or in the accrued benefit in a defined-benefit plan, he or she will still be considered covered under the plan for IRA purposes. For example, let's say that an employee is eligible for coverage under a company's defined-benefit plan with a July 1 through June 30 plan year. Then the employee decides to leave the company on December 30, 1998. Because this employee is eligible for coverage under the plan for the year ending June 30, 1999, he or she is considered covered by the plan for the 1999 tax year.

Married Individuals Don't Count Spouses' Coverage

Married individuals are treated as active participants in an employer plan *only* if they themselves are covered by their own employer's plan. This may seem obvious, but before 1998 the IRA law said that spouses of active participants were also considered active participants whether they themselves were actually covered by an employer plan or not. Today, married individuals who themselves are not covered by an employer plan may take a full $2,000 contribution deduction, even if their spouse is covered and their income exceeds the prescribed limits.

■ DEDUCTION LIMITS

As we have discussed, an individual may deduct his or her full contribution to a traditional IRA if he or she is not covered by an employer-sponsored plan at any time during the year.

An individual who *is* covered could also be entitled to a full deduction but the deduction could be reduced depending on three things:

1. income

2. filing status

3. year

The law contains a deduction *phaseout* that changes from year to year. If your client's "modified" adjusted gross income (AGI) falls below the phaseout range, he or she may deduct the entire contribution. Above the range, the deduction is zero. In between, the deduction is reduced—falling somewhere between full deductibility and zero, as described next.

Adjusted gross income generally refers to a taxpayer's gross income from all sources (including investments, retirement benefits, taxable IRA benefits, etc.) after reductions for certain items. The modification that is made to AGI for purposes of the deduction phaseout is that IRA contributions themselves are *not* subtracted in calculating modified AGI. (This avoids a circular computations that would be required if regular AGI were used.)

Figuring the Reduced IRA Deduction

IRA investors who are considered covered by an employer retirement plan must compute their deductions based on their modified AGI and tax filing status. The first thing that must be determined is the phaseout range that applies in the year of contribution. This is shown in Ill. 2.4.

The phaseout range for married individuals filing separately is $0 to $10,000 for all years, which means that few individuals will qualify for the deduction if they file separately.

AGI below phaseout range—full deduction.   If the would-be IRA investor is covered by an employer retirement plan and his or her modified AGI is below the phaseout range for the applicable filing status, he or she may take the full deduction.

AGI above phaseout range—no deduction.   If the would-be IRA investor is covered by an employer retirement plan and his or her modified AGI is above the phaseout range for the applicable filing status, he or she may not deduct any of the contribution.

AGI within phaseout range—compute reduced deduction.   If the would-be IRA investor is covered by an employer retirement plan and his or her modified AGI is within the phaseout range for the applicable filing status, the deduction is reduced.

The worksheet shown in Ill. 2.5 may be used to compute the reduced deduction.

ILL. 2.4 ■ *Phaseout Ranges*

Year	Phaseout Range for Single Individuals (Modified AGI)	Phaseout Range for Married Individuals Filing Jointly (Modified AGI)
Before 1998*	$25,000 to $35,000	$40,000 to $50,000
1998	$30,000 to $40,000	$50,000 to $60,000
1999	$31,000 to $41,000	$51,000 to $61,000
2000	$32,000 to $42,000	$52,000 to $62,000
2001	$33,000 to $43,000	$53,000 to $63,000
2002	$34,000 to $44,000	$54,000 to $64,000
2003	$40,000 to $50,000	$60,000 to $70,000
2004	$45,000 to $55,000	$65,000 to $75,000
2005	$50,000 to $60,000	$70,000 to $80,000
2006	$50,000 to $60,000	$75,000 to $85,000
2007 and after	$50,000 to $60,000	$80,000 to $100,000

*Before 1998, not only was the phaseout range less than what it was to become, but it was applied to both spouses even if only one was covered by an employer-sponsored plan. This is no longer true.

Let's look at a couple of examples.

Gary, a single taxpayer, had a modified AGI of $35,000 in 1999. He is covered under his employer's qualified retirement plan. Gary wants to limit his traditional IRA contribution to the amount that may be deducted. Gary's 1999 IRA deduction would be figured as follows:

$41,000	Top of 1999 AGI phaseout window for single individuals
−35,000	Gary's 1999 modified AGI
$ 6,000	
× .20	
$ 1,200	Gary's maximum 1999 deductible contribution

Since Gary wants to limit his IRA contribution to the maximum amount he can deduct, he would contribute $1,200. However, you could point out that Gary could contribute the $2,000 maximum, directing the nondeductible amount of $800 to a Roth IRA.

Let's look at an example with a married couple.

Susan and Dan Shapiro file their taxes jointly. Dan is an engineer and Susan is a stay-at-home mother with no income. Their modified AGI for 1999 was $57,000. Susan and Dan may each contribute $2,000 to an IRA. Susan may deduct the full amount, because she is not covered by an employer-sponsored plan (since she doesn't work). Dan is covered by his employer's plan. His deduction is figured as follows:

$61,000	Top of 1999 AGI phaseout window for joint filers
−57,000	Dan's 1999 modified AGI
$ 4,000	
× .20	
$ 800	Dan's maximum 1999 deductible contribution

The couple may, therefore, make $2,800 of deductible IRA contributions: $2,000 to Susan's IRA and $800 to Dan's. Dan could still make a $1,200 contribution to a Roth IRA. It's nondeductible, but withdrawals will be treated better than if he made nondeductible contributions to a traditional IRA.

The IRS provides worksheets in the instructions to Form 1040 to help taxpayers calculate their IRA contribution deductions.

ILL. 2.5 ■ *Worksheet: Deduction for Traditional IRAs*

1. Based on the individual's FILING STATUS and YEAR OF CONTRIBUTION, enter the top of the phaseout range. $_____

2. Enter the individual's modified AGI. $_____

3. Subtract line 2 from line 1. $_____

4a. If line 3 is $10,000* or more, STOP. The full amount of the contribution (up to $2,000) is deductible. $_____

4b. If line 3 is less than $10,000* (and more than zero), multiply line 3 by .20. Round the result to the next multiple of $10. If the result is more than $200, enter the result. Otherwise, enter $200. $_____

4c. If line 3 is zero or less, the deduction is zero. $_____

*$20,000 for joint returns after 2006.

Reporting Deductible Contributions

The deduction for IRA contributions is an above-the-line deduction, which means that IRA investors don't have to itemize deductions to claim it. (It's also why the calculation of the reduced deduction is based on modified AGI. If it were based on AGI, the calculation would be circular and unnecessarily complex.)

Individuals who wish to claim deductions for their IRA contributions must file their federal income taxes using IRS Form 1040 or 1040A (rather than the simpler Form 1040EZ). Forms 1040 and 1040A contain the necessary lines for claiming the deduction.

Nondeductible IRA Contributions

Although active participants' deductions for IRA contributions may be reduced or eliminated because of the AGI limitation, they may still make contributions of up to $2,000 ($4,000 for a regular and spousal IRA combined) or 100 percent of compensation, whichever is less.

The difference between total permitted contributions and total deductible contributions, if any, is the "nondeductible contribution." It may be made to a traditional IRA or, if the investor qualifies, to a Roth IRA.

For instance, take the situation of Ken, who is single and covered by an employer retirement plan. In 1999, his modified AGI was $46,235. Ken wants to make a $2,000 IRA contribution for 1999. Ken may not deduct any of his 1999 contribution because he is covered by his employer's retirement plan *and* his modified AGI was more than $41,000.

Although Ken is not entitled to a tax deduction for his contribution, making an IRA contribution is not without an important tax advantage. Assuming Ken's contributions are within the limits, none of the earnings on his nondeductible contributions will be taxed until they are distributed.

This is true of both a traditional IRA and a Roth IRA. With a Roth IRA, however, qualifying withdrawals are received entirely tax free. This is not true of a traditional IRA. Because of this difference, eligible individuals would always be better off making nondeductible contributions to a Roth IRA. However, not all individuals are eligible for this option.

In a traditional IRA, withdrawals are taxed *except* for the portion that represents a return of nondeductible contributions. This is referred to as "basis" or "cost basis" and is returned to the investor tax free.

The IRS has rules that treats a portion of each withdrawal as coming from nondeductible contributions and the remainder as coming from deductible contributions and earnings—until all basis is recovered. From that point on, any withdrawals would not include any basis and would therefore be fully taxable.

Reporting Nondeductible Contributions

Although IRA owners must report their nondeductible contributions, they do not have to specify a contribution as nondeductible until they actually file their tax returns.

To designate contributions as nondeductible, IRA owners must file Form 8606, "Nondeductible IRAs (Contributions, Distributions and Basis)." Form 8606 is generally used by a taxpayer who makes nondeductible contributions to an IRA and also when a taxpayer receives distributions and once made nondeductible contributions to any IRA.

Taxpayers may think it is not necessary to report nondeductible IRA contributions. But failure to report nondeductible contributions, will result in certain consequences. First, all of the unreported IRA contributions will be treated as deductible, and when the IRA owner makes withdrawals from his or her IRA, the withdrawn amounts will be fully taxed unless he or she can prove to the IRS that nondeductible contributions were actually made.

Second, the IRS will impose a $50 penalty on taxpayers who do not file the required Form 8606, unless they can prove that the failure to file was due to a reasonable cause. A penalty will also be assessed for overstatement of the amount of nondeductible contributions. There is a $100 penalty for each overstatement, unless the taxpayer can show that the error was due to reasonable cause.

■ TAKING MONEY OUT OF A TRADITIONAL IRA

There are two things you should know about withdrawals from traditional IRAs. First, withdrawals are taxable (mostly). Second, preretirement withdrawals may be subject to a 10 percent penalty *in addition to* the tax.

Let's take the first point first. Funds that have been sheltered from tax in an IRA are taxed fully when they are withdrawn. This includes deductible contributions and investment earnings. Only withdrawals that come from nondeductible contributions may be taken tax free.

Does this mean that an IRA investor has a choice in labeling his or her withdrawals as coming from nondeductible contributions (if they ever were made)? No, the IRS has rules about this. IRA owners are required to compare the amount of nondeductible contributions ever made to the total value of the account (or accounts). If nondeductible contributions represent 23 percent of the account, then 23 percent of the withdrawal is tax free. The rest is fully taxable. As you will see in the next chapter, this is quite different from the Roth IRA.

Now, let's look at the early withdrawal penalty. IRAs are meant to be retirement accounts, so Congress has imposed a serious penalty of 10 percent on most withdrawals taken before the IRA owner reaches age 59½. This penalty is paid in addition to tax. If the IRA owner is unemployed and has no income, the cost of a withdrawal may be limited to the 10 percent. But if the IRA owner has significant income, the penalty may make an early withdrawal prohibitive. For example, if your client is in the 39 percent tax bracket, he or she would have to pay the IRS 49 percent of the withdrawal (39 percent tax plus 10 percent penalty).

Over the years, many people shied away from investing in an IRA for just this reason. They liked the tax advantages offered by the arrangement, but didn't want to subject themselves to this withdrawal penalty if they had an emergency need for funds.

The Taxpayer Relief Act of 1997 changed all that (with some help from earlier legislation). Penalty-free withdrawals now may be used for many of the family needs investors are concerned with. The penalty has been dropped if the withdrawal is used to purchase a first home, to pay for education or to pay deductible medical expenses. Other exceptions to the penalty apply if the IRA owner dies, is disabled or takes the distribution in the form of a life annuity. Details on these rules appear in Chapter 4.

Whether the penalty applies or not, however, these distributions are generally subject to regular tax. This is the downside of a traditional IRA. The investor has enjoyed tax deferral for many years, but the time comes when the tax has to be paid.

This inexorable logic has led people who don't have immediate need for the funds to postpone withdrawals for as long as possible. Once an IRA owner reaches the age of 70½, however, withdrawals from a traditional IRA must begin. These complicated rules (which don't apply to Roth IRAs since Roth IRA withdrawals are not taxed anyway) are also discussed in detail in Chapter 4.

■ SUMMARY

In this chapter you have learned how to figure the amount an individual may contribute to a traditional IRA and the amount they may deduct. For most, the annual contribution is $2,000 (less if the investor or spouse has less in compensation for the year). This amount is generally deductible, but investors who are covered by an employer-sponsored retirement plan may have their deductions limited or eliminated if their incomes exceed IRS limits.

The key advantage of a traditional IRA is tax deferral. Investment earnings are not taxed while in the IRA. This advantage coupled with deductible contributions (if applicable) magnify the amount an investor may save for retirement.

IRAs have taken on a new life. Before 1998, IRAs were seen by many as a nice-to-have but inessential ingredient in an individual's financial plan. This was due to two facts. First, many people were precluded from deducting IRA contributions because they or their spouses were covered by employer-sponsored retirement plans. This restriction has been eased considerably.

Second, some people were reluctant to tie up their money in an IRA because withdrawals for most preretirement needs were subject to a 10 percent penalty that would have to be paid on top of any tax that would be due. This restriction, too, has been eased. Now your clients may make penalty-free withdrawals for certain medical, education and first-time home-buying expenses.

The landscape for your client, then, is this: There are two basic varieties of IRA—traditional IRAs and Roth IRAs. This chapter has covered the traditional IRA and both deductible and nondeductible contributions. All three (Roth, deductible, and nondeductible) have important uses. And the choice between them depends on whether your client is covered by an employer plan, your client's current tax bracket and his or her projected tax bracket at the time of retirement. How the choice is made is discussed in the next chapter.

■ CHAPTER 2 QUESTIONS FOR REVIEW

1. Which of the following items would NOT be considered "compensation" for IRA purposes?

   A. Tips

   B. Salary

   C. Commissions from sales

   D. Interest earned on a bank certificate of deposit

2. Eric Armstrong earned $1,000 from his job as a waiter last year. He had no other compensation. What is the maximum IRA contribution that Eric can make to an IRA for that year?

   A. $250

   B. $1,000

   C. $2,000

   D. $2,250

3. Last year Carol and John Crabtree, a married couple, jointly earned $75,000. Mary is an active participant in her employer's qualified retirement plan. If John, who is self-employed, wishes to contribute to an IRA, that contribution will be

   A. fully deductible

   B. partially deductible

   C. nondeductible

   D. conditionally deductible

4. Hannah Stone contributed $2,000 to an IRA on April 14, 1999. To which tax year may this contribution be credited?

   A. 1998

   B. 1999

   C. Any year that Hannah designates

   D. Hannah may designate either 1998 or 1999

5. Forrest and Jackie Green contributed $4,000 to two IRAs (one for him and one for her) in 1999. Forrest is covered by his employer's retirement plan. Jackie is not employed. Forrest's income is $85,000 for the year. How much can the couple deduct if they file joint tax returns?

   A. $0

   B. $2,000

   C. $2,250

   D. $4,000

3

Roth IRAs

For more than 20 years, traditional IRAs have helped people increase their retirement savings by deferring tax on investment earnings and, for some, by giving a deduction at the time contributions are made. The tax savings comes at the beginning, but sooner or later the IRS has to be paid. So every distribution is treated as income subject to tax.

A new option was introduced in 1998 called the "Roth IRA," named after Sen. William V. Roth, Jr., a long-time advocate of IRAs. This type of IRA "backloads" the tax savings. Instead of giving a deduction when contributions are made, the Roth IRA eliminates the tax on qualifying distributions.

In this chapter, you will learn exactly what it means to backload IRA tax savings, how a Roth IRA works and who is eligible to open one. Roth IRAs are advantageous for many people, but not all. In this chapter, you will begin to compare the advantages of a Roth IRA with those of a traditional IRA and consider the circumstances that would dictate investment in one type or another.

■ ■ ■ ■ ■

■ HOW A ROTH IRA WORKS

First, lets look at the similarity between the two types of IRA. Regardless of type, earnings on investments held in an IRA are not taxed.

In a traditional IRA, the tax-free condition is temporary. Earnings are not taxed until funds are withdrawn. Then they are taxed. This is called *tax deferral*. In a Roth IRA, the tax-free condition is permanent. This is not tax deferral. It is *tax exemption*. Once your client puts money into a Roth IRA, there is no more tax (unless withdrawals are made counter to the rules that we will discuss later in this chapter).

In the life of an IRA, there are three basic "opportunities" for tax savings. We've talked about tax savings at the time contributions are made to the IRA (one) and tax savings for the duration of the IRA investment (two). This describes a traditional

IRA, which allows eligible individuals to take a deduction for a contribution. The third opportunity for tax savings occurs at the time of withdrawal. This is the opportunity offered by the Roth IRA, which allows tax-free withdrawals.

Simply put, each type of IRA offers tax savings at two of the three tax-savings opportunities, but not all three. For traditional IRAs, the savings comes at the beginning and the duration of the investment. For Roth IRAs the savings comes during the investment and at the end. But the best way to understand how a Roth IRA compares to a traditional IRA is to see it in action.

Let's say that Louise budgets $2,000 a year for retirement savings. She has three options: she can invest the money outside of an IRA, in a traditional IRA or in a Roth IRA. Let's see how much Louise can expect to have when she retires. We'll assume she is in the 28 percent tax bracket now and that she will be in the same bracket when she retires in 20 years. She is eligible to deduct contributions to a traditional IRA, which will be an important point in our comparison later on.

	Regular Savings	Traditional IRA	Roth IRA
Annual deposit	$2,000	$2,000	$2,000
Value of the account after 20 years	$75,824	$91,524	$91,524
Tax on withdrawal	$0	$25,627	$0
Net retirement savings	$75,824	$65,897*	$91,524

* The $65,897 figure for the traditional IRA does not include the value of the $2,000 she could deduct from her taxes each year for 20 years.

Regular savings.   If Louise puts her money into regular savings, her earnings will be taxed as she goes along. This is reflected in the $75,824 value of her account after 20 years. As you can see, the tax-free growth in both types of IRA yields more than $15,000 extra (in pre-withdrawal value) after the same amount of time.

IRA options.   Both IRA options start well ahead of regular savings, but Louise has to pay tax on every penny when she withdraws the money from the traditional IRA. This leaves the Roth IRA way ahead and the traditional IRA way behind regular savings.

But something is wrong with this picture. Regular savings should not come out ahead of an IRA (all other things being equal). What's missing?

Value of the deduction.   The thing missing here is the deduction Louise gets for contributing to a traditional IRA. In the 28 percent bracket, the deduction gives her $560 back each year, which she doesn't get with the Roth IRA (because the Roth IRA is nondeductible). If Louise invests this tax savings (not in an IRA, because she's already made the maximum contribution—but at the same pre-tax rate of interest), she'll have an additional $21,231 when she retires. Add this to the $65,897 she got from her IRA and Louise has $87,128—much better than regular savings and almost as good as the Roth IRA.

Does this mean that Roth IRAs are better than traditional IRAs? Not always. We assumed that Louise was in the 28 percent bracket. If her tax bracket drops to 15 percent when she retires, which is often the case, the story is different. Now Louise's savings with the traditional IRA—after tax—is $99,026, because she's paying less tax when she withdraws the money. The figure for the Roth IRA doesn't change, because there's no tax on withdrawal. So, in this second scenario Louise would do better with a traditional IRA. It's all a matter of tax brackets and your ability to predict them.

■ WHO IS ELIGIBLE TO OPEN A ROTH IRA?

Like traditional IRAs, Roth IRAs may be opened by anyone with compensation sufficient to cover the contribution, up to $2,000. Nonworking spouses may rely on the working spouse's income if the couple files joint returns. The rules are exactly the same as with a traditional IRA. The difference between the two types of IRA enters at the high end of income.

Roth IRAs are generally available to more people than are deductible IRAs. Why is this? Roth IRAs are available to individuals regardless of whether they are covered by employer-sponsored plans or not. This makes Roth IRAs particularly attractive to people who have retirement coverage at work.

Roth IRAs are not universally available, however. Investors with high incomes do not have the choice to open an IRA. Eligibility is phased out for married individuals filing jointly with combined incomes between $150,000 and $160,000. The phaseout for single individual is $95,000 to $110,000. Illustration 3.2 shows the choices available for individuals covered by an employer-sponsored plan.

■ TAKING MONEY OUT OF A ROTH IRA

Traditional IRAs have fairly complicated rules about distributions including penalties for early and late distributions. The structure is much simpler for a Roth IRA, as you will see here and in the chapter on distributions.

Why the difference? The reason has to do with the distinction between tax exemption and tax deferral. With a Roth IRA an investor has already paid all the tax he or she is going to pay. That means that he or she took no deduction for contributions, but withdrawals will probably be tax free. The IRS really has a fairly minimal ongoing interest in a Roth IRA. There's probably no future tax to collect. So the rules are fairly simple.

A traditional IRA is different. Every deductible contribution implies an obligation to pay future taxes to the IRS. Every dollar withdrawn from a traditional IRA is taxable (except if nondeductible contributions were ever made). This difference is the main reason the rules about distributions from a traditional IRA are much more complicated than for a Roth IRA. Chapter 4 discusses distributions in detail. Here we're going to outline just the rules for Roths.

ILL. 3.1 ◼ *Is A Traditional or Roth IRA Better?*

This is the big question and the answer is: It depends.

Eligibility to Invest in a Roth IRA

Upper-income clients may not be eligible for a Roth IRA. Married investors who file joint returns are ineligible for a Roth if their combined incomes exceed $160,000. Single investors are out of the Roth game if their incomes exceed $110,000. These investors are forced to open traditional IRAs if they want an IRA at all.

Eligibility to Make Deductible Contributions

The big plus for a traditional IRA is the deduction for contributions. If your client is covered by an employer-sponsored retirement plan and his or her income exceeds the phaseout range, he or she is not entitled to take the deduction. So the big benefit of the traditional IRA is lost. This type of client should invest in a Roth IRA.

Can Your Client Make Use of the Deduction?

An investor who puts $2,000 a year into an IRA will always have more at withdrawal time by investing in a Roth. But this ignores the value of the deduction that can come from investing in a traditional IRA. If your client can invest the resulting tax savings outside of an IRA, he or she may be able to augment the traditional IRA sufficiently to make it competitive with a Roth. If the client can't do this, he or she should invest in a Roth.

Which Tax Bracket Will Apply When Your Client Retires?

The big negative for the traditional IRA is that retirement withdrawals are fully taxed. This is not true with a Roth IRA. Will this be a problem for your client? It depends on how much income the client expects at retirement. Under the current system of tax brackets, many middle-class retirees are in the 15 percent bracket, but your clients might expect more income at retirement than the average. At 15 percent the tax on traditional IRA withdrawals may be low enough to tip the scale the other way, making the Roth IRA less desirable. But at higher rates, the Roth can produce a larger amount of after-tax savings.

Here is a chart to help your client decide which type of IRA to buy. It's based on the assumption that your client invests (in a taxable investment) the tax saving resulting from deducting the traditional IRA contributions.

Tax Bracket, Time of Contribution	Tax Bracket at Retirement				
	15%	28%	31%	36%	39.6%
15%	Roth	Roth	Roth	Roth	Roth
28%	Traditional	Roth	Roth	Roth	Roth
31%	Traditional	Roth	Roth	Roth	Roth
36%	Traditional	Roth, if eligible	Roth, if eligible	Roth, if eligible	Roth, if eligible
39.6%	Traditional*	Traditional*	Traditional*	Traditional*	Traditional*

* Investors in the 39.6% bracket are ineligible for a Roth IRA.

ILL. 3.1 ■ *Is A Traditional or Roth IRA Better? (Continued)*

Is Your Client's Contribution Contingent Upon Getting a Deduction?

Some clients can't make the full $2,000 contribution without getting a deduction. If that is the case, a traditional IRA may be appropriate in circumstances when it would not be if the client had the full $2,000 to invest. In such a case, a Roth (with a reduced contribution) would yield a greater nest egg only if the client expects to be in a higher tax bracket at retirement than now. (If the client expects to be in the same tax bracket, the question is a toss-up, and should be based on other features of the two types of IRA.)

Consider Preretirement Withdrawals

We've talked a lot about your client's tax bracket after retirement. But the new IRAs allow certain types of withdrawals before retirement. If your client will need to make any preretirement withdrawals—for a home or education—make sure that the IRA he or she opens has the flexibility to meet those needs.

Your Client's Choice Is Not Forever

Rules of thumb, like the one illustrated here, simplify the analysis needed to choose between the two types of IRA. The complicated part is projecting your client's future tax bracket. Even if you are able to project income, there's no telling how law changes will affect future tax brackets.

The good thing is that your client is not limited to owning one type of IRA. As current circumstances change, you might recommend a Roth IRA one year when your client's income is modest and a traditional IRA the next, when your client's income rises and he or she needs a deduction. Or you might make changes as the picture of your client's retirement resources becomes clearer. The only limit is that the total contribution for a single year may not exceed $2,000. Beyond that, you may mix and match to tailor a program to your client's needs.

Roth IRAs Are Not Just for Retirement

The year 1998 became a watershed in the history of IRAs when many of the restrictions on preretirement withdrawals were significantly liberalized. Before that time, IRA investors paid a hefty 10 percent penalty in addition to tax for most distributions before age 59½. Traditional IRAs carry a much less restrictive burden now than they did as recently as 1997. But Roth IRAs are more liberal yet.

The most liberal rules apply to withdrawals know as "qualified distributions." These are withdrawals made for one of the following reasons if taken at least five years after contributions were made:

1. reaching age 59½ (the retirement option);

2. death of the owner (distribution to the owner's beneficiary or estate);

3. disability of the owner; and

4. purchase of a first home (up to $10,000 of qualified expenses).

ILL. 3.2   *IRA Options Depend on Income Level and Coverage by Employer-Sponsored Retirement Plan*

No Coverage at Work
Determining eligibility for the different types of IRA is relatively simple if the investor is not covered by an employer-sponsored retirement plan. There is no limit on eligibility for a deductible IRA and eligibility for a Roth IRA is phased out for single taxpayers with incomes between $95,000 and $110,000 and for married taxpayers filing jointly with combined incomes between $150,000 and $160,000. Above that level, only a traditional IRA may be used.

Coverage at Work
Investors who are covered by an employer-sponsored plan have their choices set based upon their income level as shown.

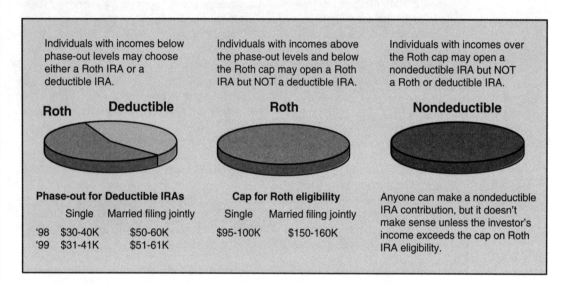

Individuals with incomes below phase-out levels may choose either a Roth IRA or a deductible IRA.

Individuals with incomes above the phase-out levels and below the Roth cap may open a Roth IRA but NOT a deductible IRA.

Individuals with incomes over the Roth cap may open a nondeductible IRA but NOT a Roth or deductible IRA.

Roth   Deductible

Roth

Nondeductible

Phase-out for Deductible IRAs

	Single	Married filing jointly
'98	$30-40K	$50-60K
'99	$31-41K	$51-61K

Cap for Roth eligibility

Single	Married filing jointly
$95-100K	$150-160K

Anyone can make a nondeductible IRA contribution, but it doesn't make sense unless the investor's income exceeds the cap on Roth IRA eligibility.

Spouse's Participation in an Employer Plan Does Not Matter
Before 1998, an investor could be shut out of a deductible IRA if his or her spouse were covered by a retirement plan at work. This is no longer true. Each spouse figures eligibility separately.

But that's not the end of the story. Remember that Roth IRAs hold after-tax money (that is, there was no tax deduction for contributions). This is different than traditional IRAs, which hold pre-tax money.

Under Roth IRA rules, the investor may withdraw all of his or her contributions at any time without incurring any tax liability. As long as total withdrawals are less than the total of all contributions to the account, there's no tax.

This means that a Roth IRA can be used as a growing source of funds—for any reason. The amount is limited only by the total amount of contributions made up to the date of withdrawal. These are called "nonqualified distributions." But just remember that, in this case, it may not be bad to be nonqualified.

How a Nonqualified Distribution Works

Barry opened a Roth IRA in 1998 (the first year they became available). He contributed the maximum $2,000 each year. After four years his account was worth $11,800, of which $8,000 represented four years of accumulated contributions. At that point, Barry could withdraw up to $8,000 tax free.

If he withdraws any more than $8,000, the excess is taxed. So if Barry withdraws $9,500, he gets $8,000 tax free (because the contributions were after tax) and he pays tax on the remaining $1,500.

The $1,500 is also subject to a 10 percent early withdrawal penalty if taken before age 59½ unless taken for first-time home purchases (up to $10,000) or qualified education or medical expenses. Substantially equal periodic payments over the life of the owner—or owner and beneficiary—are also exempt from penalty, but not tax.

■ SUMMARY

This chapter has focused on the differences between traditional and Roth IRAs. These are the factors you must know in order to guide your client to make an intelligent choice between the two. But many aspects of the two types of IRAs are identical. Illustrations 3.3 and 3.4 summarize, respectively, the similarities and the differences between Roth IRAs and traditional IRAs.

■ CHAPTER 3 QUESTIONS FOR REVIEW

1. Lester Crockett has contributed the maximum to his Roth IRA every year since 1998. At the end of 2001, Lester decides to take a world cruise in honor of his 30th birthday. The account is worth $15,000 at that time. How much can he withdraw without paying any taxes on the withdrawal?

    A. $0
    B. $2,000
    C. $8,000
    D. $15,000

2. Nick and Sarah Good have a combined income of $170,000 in 1999. How much can they contribute to their Roth IRAs for that year?

    A. $0
    B. $1,000
    C. $2,000
    D. $4,000

ILL. 3.3 ■ *Similarities Between Roth IRAs and Traditional IRAs*

Contribution Limits

Maximum total contribution to all IRAs is $2,000 per year. Limit is reduced if IRA investor has less than $2,000 in earned income.

Nonworking Spouse

Nonworking spouses may make contributions of up to $2,000 per year if working spouse has earned income. (This is subject to phase out between $150,000 and $160,000 of income. Eligibility is phased out for Roth IRAs. Deduction is phased out for traditional IRAs.)

Compensation

Contributions must be made out of compensation (of the investor or spouse), which includes pay from employers, self-employment income and taxable alimony.

Contribution Deadlines

Contributions may be made at any time during the year. Late contributions are accepted through April 15 following the year (but must be designated as applying to the previous year rather than the current year). Early contributions are preferable so that the funds have longer to grow.

Investment Options

Both types of IRAs may be invested in securities, mutual funds and annuities. Both are restricted from investments such as real estate and collectibles.

Tax on Earnings

Funds held in an IRA accumulate earnings (interest, dividends, capital gains) without incurring tax.

Penalty on Early Withdrawal

There is a 10 percent early withdrawal penalty tax that applies (in addition to regular tax) to taxable withdrawals taken before age 59½ other than the following: distributions made at death or disability, distributions made for certain health expenses, education expenses or first-time home purchases, and substantially equal periodic payments made for the life (lives) of the recipient(s). (Note that withdrawals of Roth IRA contributions are not subject to this penalty because they are not taxable.)

ILL. 3.4 ■ *Differences Between Roth IRAs and Traditional IRAs*

	Roth IRA	Traditional IRA
Eligibility	Eligibility to contribute to a Roth IRA is phased out between $150,000 and $160,000 of income. Individuals with incomes above that range may not contribute to a Roth IRA.	There is no maximum income for contributions to a traditional IRA.
Deductibility of Contributions	Contributions are not deductible.	Contributions are deductible unless the IRA investor is covered by an employer retirement plan and has income over the phaseout range. Nondeductible contributions may be made.
Taxation of Distributions	Distributions are tax free if the account has been held at least five years and the money is taken after age 59½ on account of death or disability or for the purchase of a first home (up to $10,000). Before that, contributions (but not earnings) may be withdrawn tax free.	Distributions are taxed, except for any portion that comes from nondeductible contributions.
Required Distributions	No distributions are required.	Distributions must begin after the investor reaches age 70½.
Contributions After Age 70½	Permitted.	Not permitted.

3. Which of the following is TRUE for a Roth IRA but FALSE for a traditional IRA?

   A. Contributions may be deductible.

   B. Contributions may be withdrawn at any time without being subject to tax.

   C. Withdrawals taken after the account has been held for five years are taxed at capital gains rates.

   D. Withdrawals taken to make a qualified purchase of a first home are not subject to penalties.

4. Jake Darling set up a Roth IRA, but died after three years. His wife Kathy was his beneficiary and would like to withdraw all the money. What can she withdraw without paying taxes?

   A. Kathy may withdraw Jake's contributions, but she must wait until the account reaches its fifth year before withdrawing any earnings tax free.

   B. Kathy must pay tax on the full amount of any withdrawal.

   C. Kathy may take the entire amount free of tax.

   D. Kathy may not withdraw the money.

5. All of the following are true of a Roth IRA EXCEPT

   A. funds may be withdrawn tax free after age 59½ if the account has been held five years

   B. contributions to the IRA are not deductible

   C. contributions may be deducted if the investor is not an active participant in an employer's retirement plan

   D. earnings on IRA investments are not subject to tax while in the IRA

4

Taking Money Out of an IRA

A lthough the main purpose of an IRA is to provide the investor with retirement income, many people want their IRA funds to be available to meet other needs. This desire was not easily met during the first 20 years of IRA history. An array of withdrawal penalties restricted planning flexibility. Today, the penalties still exist, but a number of exceptions have been enacted to meet many people's needs.

Today, too, there is more than one type of IRA. Some of the complexity of distribution rules apply to all IRAs. Some apply to one type or another. In particular, traditional IRAs are subject to the most complex distribution rules. Rules about Roth IRA distributions are simple by comparison.

Before we get into the specifics of the IRA distribution rules, however, it pays to consider some of the reasons why distribution rules differ between traditional and Roth IRAs.

- The first reason centers around the distinction between tax *deferral* and tax *exemption.* A traditional IRA *defers* tax, but the tax is paid eventually when the money is withdrawn. A Roth IRA *exempts* income from tax. Once minimum requirements are met, withdrawals are tax free.

  With a Roth, the investor has already paid the tax and is not required to pay again if minimum requirements are met. With a traditional IRA, if the investor got a deduction for his or her contribution, he or she is expected to pay for that deduction when the money is withdrawn. If a deduction for contributions was not taken, no taxes will be assessed when the contributions are withdrawn; however, the *earnings* that have accumulated are subject to tax when they are ultimately withdrawn.

  This means that the IRS is very interested in traditional IRAs (so they can collect the tax) but has only a slight interest in Roths (because no tax is due). That's one reason why distribution rules focus heavily on traditional IRAs.

- The second reason is a kind of practical/political one. At the time Roth IRAs were introduced in the 1997 tax legislation, billions of dollars were already invested in traditional IRAs. It would have been very difficult to make sweeping changes in the rules for existing accounts. Instead, Congress created the new Roth IRA and allowed some investors to convert traditional IRAs into Roths if they wanted to come under the new rules. But of course there's a catch. As you will see in Chapter 5, an investor who converts to a Roth IRA has to pay the tax now (or over four years if the conversion takes place in 1998).

  The other side of this coin is that investments in Roth IRAs only began in 1998. This means that the first *qualified* withdrawals won't come until 2003 (after the five-year holding period). And really large withdrawals (except in the case of rollovers or conversions) won't come until years after that.

IRAs can become one of the largest assets an individual owns. A financial representative, therefore, has to be prepared to discuss the most common types of distribution options available with his or her client. Moreover, as Roth IRAs grow over the years, many investors may have funds invested in more than one type of IRA.

The question from younger IRA owners will be: "I need to make a withdrawal for such-and-such a purpose. Should I take it from my traditional IRA or my Roth?" The question from older and more well-to-do IRA owners will be "I don't have an immediate need, can I keep my money in my IRAs and still reap the tax benefits?" The answer, of course, depends on the type of IRA held.

The purpose of this chapter is to help a financial representative answer questions like these. First you'll learn about preretirement withdrawals, then retirement withdrawals and, finally, withdrawals by beneficiaries who inherit IRAs. You'll also learn about required distributions, a concept that applies only to traditional IRAs.

■ ■ ■ ■ ■

■ TAKING MONEY OUT BEFORE AGE 59½

IRAs are intended mainly for retirement. Although the retirement angle has been lessened by recent legislation that allows withdrawals for other purposes, it's still the principal focus. And it's enforced by a penalty: if an investor withdraws money from an IRA before age 59½, there's a 10 percent penalty tax that has to be paid on top of any regular tax that might be due.

This is true of *taxable* distributions from both traditional and Roth IRAs. An IRA investor in the 28 percent tax bracket could pay 38 percent on a withdrawal taken before age 59½. An investor in the 39 percent bracket could lose almost half (49 percent) of the withdrawal to taxes. This kind of penalty is a real incentive for an investor to keep money in the IRA until retirement.

For many, however, there are exceptions to the penalty that allow penalty-free (and sometime tax-free) preretirement withdrawals for:

- a first-time home purchase;
- deductible medical expenses;

- health insurance premiums for the unemployed;

- education expenses for the investor and family members;

- death or disability;

- any reason, if taken out of contributions accumulated in a Roth (the Roth "exception") but not earnings; and

- any reason, if taken as a life annuity.

How these exceptions are applied are discussed in the pages that follow.

The Roth "Exception"

Let's take a look at the Roth "exception" first, since all the rest of the exceptions apply to both types—and because it is the ultimate in IRA flexibility.

The idea here is that the Roth IRA investor can get contributions back tax free at any time. This is not like the rule that allows a traditional IRA investor to withdraw contributions before the due date of his tax return—discussed later in this chapter. The right to withdraw contributions tax free continues forever.

This means that the tax and penalty that applies to IRA withdrawals, in the case of a Roth IRA, applies only to withdrawals of earnings. As discussed in Chapter 3, as long as a Roth IRA investor limits withdrawals to the amount contributed, there is no tax or penalty. Once the investor goes beyond that amount, withdrawals are subject to the same rules that apply to withdrawals from a traditional IRA.

This is a nice rule for investors who would be leery about tying up their money for as long as IRAs can exist before the penalty is lifted (say, from age 30 to age 59½). They can always get their contributions back. On the other hand, once contributions are withdrawn, they may never be replaced.

Special Purpose Withdrawals

For qualifying special purpose withdrawals, there is no 10 percent early withdrawal penalty. There may be tax, however, depending on the type of IRA involved.

- **Traditional IRA.** If no nondeductible contributions were ever made to the investor's traditional IRA, the special purpose withdrawal is fully taxable (but, remember, no penalty). If nondeductible contributions *were* made, part of the distribution may escape tax under rules discussed later in this chapter under the heading "Fully or Partially Taxable Distributions."

- **Roth IRA.** Special purpose withdrawals (except for home purchase withdrawals) may generate taxable income but, as with a traditional IRA, no penalty. The taxable portion of the withdrawal is determined following the "Roth Exception" rule we just discussed. The withdrawal comes first from contributions and is tax free. Only withdrawals from earnings are taxed.

ILL. 4.1 ■ *Use and Abuse of Unrestricted Withdrawals of Roth IRA Contributions*

Although the unrestricted tax-free withdrawal of Roth IRA contributions is a nice feature, there are some potential pitfalls that a financial representative should be aware of.

Let's say that Barry Boone, age 25, started contributing to a Roth IRA in 1998. If he made the maximum $2,000 contributions for 20 years and earned 10 percent, he would have approximately $115,000 in 2018. Out of this amount, $40,000 would represent total contributions. The rest would be attributable to earnings.

But Barry is not the type who forgets that the money is there. Since he can withdraw contributions tax free, he does so periodically until, in 2017 (year 19), his accumulated withdrawals total $38,000. That's all he's ever contributed.

At this point, he can't take any more unrestricted tax-free withdrawals. He's used up his contributions. Additional withdrawals will be taxed and subject to the 10 percent penalty.

Unfortunately, tax-free withdrawals may not be repaid. Once a Roth IRA investor withdraws contributions, they stay withdrawn. Every withdrawal means not only that the amount withdrawn is gone from the account but that all future tax-free growth of the withdrawal is also gone.

When Barry hit zero in accumulated contributions in 2017, he decided not to "dip into earnings." The next year he made his regular $2,000 contribution. At the end of 2018, his account was worth $36,348, which is $78,652 less than he would have had if he had never made the withdrawals. His withdrawals cost him over $40,000 in additional earnings.

Since withdrawals may not be replaced, every one is a lost opportunity.

Qualifying withdrawals for a first-time home purchase may escape tax altogether if the IRA has been held for five years. (This is the same rule that applies to withdrawals made after age 59½ or upon death or disability, as we will discuss later.)

What are qualifying special purpose withdrawals? There are four types:

1. **First-time home purchase**. An IRA investor may withdraw up to a lifetime total of $10,000 for qualified first-time home-purchase expenses of the investor; the investor's spouse; or their children, grandchildren, parents or grandparents. These include the cost of the property and settlement, financing, or other closing costs. Although most people acquire a *first* home only once, the Tax Code allows a person to acquire a first home *again* if there has been a two-year gap in home ownership. The real limit on the use of this exception is the $10,000 lifetime cap, which is applied to the IRA investor.

2. **Education expenses**. To qualify for the education-expense exception, a distribution must be used for tuition, fees, books, supplies or equipment required to college, graduate school or some other post-secondary educational institution. The expenses may be incurred by the IRA investor; the investor's spouse; or their children, grandchildren, parents, or grandparents. Expenses that are paid by scholarships are not included.

3. **Deductible medical expenses**. The third exception to the 10 percent penalty (and—as with the others—to taxation altogether for Roth IRAs held for five years) is withdrawals to pay for deductible medical expenses. This includes any medical expense that could count toward the IRA investor's itemized deductions (whether he or she itemizes or not). This means paying for the health care of the investor, the investor's spouse and any dependents.

4. **Health insurance for the unemployed**. The final special purpose exception applies to withdrawals made by an unemployed IRA investor that are used to pay health insurance premiums.

Disability or Death Exceptions

If IRA investors become disabled before reaching age 59½, they may withdraw amounts from their IRAs without having to pay the 10 percent penalty. In the case of a Roth IRA held for at least five years, the withdrawals will also be tax free.

The IRS will consider a taxpayer to be disabled for IRA distribution purposes if he or she cannot do "any substantial gainful activity" because of a physical or mental condition. A physician must certify that the condition has lasted, or can be expected to last, continuously for 12 months or more or that the condition can be expected to result in earlier death. (This definition of disability mirrors the one used to determine eligibility for Social Security disability benefits.)

If an IRA investor dies before becoming age 59½, the assets in his or her IRA may be distributed to a named beneficiary or to the IRA owner's estate without being subject to the 10 percent additional tax. Again, in the case of a Roth IRA held for at least five years, the withdrawals will also be tax free.

If a surviving spouse inherits an IRA from a deceased spouse and elects to treat it as his or her own, then the surviving spouse will face the 10 percent penalty for any distribution he or she might subsequently take before reaching age 59½.

The Annuity Exception

If IRA investors are willing to receive distributions from their IRAs very slowly, they might be able to avoid the 10 percent penalty tax, even if those distributions begin before the IRA owner becomes age 59½.

An investor may receive distributions from an IRA that are part of a series of substantially equal payments over his or her life (or life expectancy), or over the lives (or life expectancies) of both the IRA owner and his or her beneficiary. An IRS-approved distribution method must be used and the IRA investor must receive at least one distribution per year for this exception to apply. The IRS-approved

ILL. 4.2 *Comparing IRA Early Withdrawals—Traditional vs. Roth*

How preretirement withdrawals are treated may be a significant question for a would-be IRA investor. One investor may have no reason to expect taking withdrawals prior to age 59½. Another may not feel secure putting money into an IRA without assurance that the money will be available if a need arises. The following chart compares the treatment of various kinds of preretirement withdrawals from the two main types of IRA: traditional and Roth.

Type of Withdrawal	Traditional IRA	Roth IRA
First-time home purchase (up to $10,000)	No penalty. Distribution taxed (except fraction due to non-deductible contributions).	No penalty. No tax if held for five years—otherwise, distribution taxed to the extent it exceeds accumulated contributions.
Educational expenses	No penalty. Distribution taxed (except fraction due to non-deductible contributions).	No penalty. Distribution taxed to the extent it exceeds accumulated contributions.
Medical expenses (deductible)	No penalty. Distribution taxed (except fraction due to non-deductible contributions).	No penalty. Distribution taxed to the extent it exceeds accumulated contributions.
Health insurance premiums (for unemployed)	No penalty. Distribution taxed (except fraction due to non-deductible contributions).	No penalty. Distribution taxed to the extent it exceeds accumulated contributions.
Disability	No penalty. Distribution taxed (except fraction due to non-deductible contributions).	No penalty. No tax if held for five years—otherwise, distribution taxed to the extent it exceeds accumulated contributions.
Death	No penalty. Distribution taxed (except fraction due to non-deductible contributions).	No penalty (but penalty may apply if beneficiary spouse converts IRA to own account). No tax if held for five years—otherwise, distribution taxed to the extent it exceeds accumulated contributions.
Life annuity	No penalty. Distribution taxed (except fraction due to non-deductible contributions).	No penalty. No tax if held for five years—otherwise, distribution taxed to the extent it exceeds accumulated contributions.
Any reason not listed	Penalty applies to taxable amount. Distribution taxed (except fraction due to non-deductible contributions).	Penalty applies to taxable amount. Investor may withdraw contributions without tax or penalty. Withdrawals from earnings are subject to both.

distribution method will not determine a minimum distribution; rather, it will be used to calculate the *exact* amount required to be distributed each period.

The payments under this annuity exception must continue for either five years or until the IRA owner reaches age 59½, whichever is longer. This five-year rule does not apply if a change from an IRS-approved distribution method is a result of the death or disability of the IRA owner.

If the payments under this exception are changed for any reason other than death or disability of the IRA owner, the 10 percent penalty tax will be imposed. This penalty applies, of course, only to the taxable portion of the payment. Where after-tax contributions have been made, as in the case of a Roth IRA or nondeductible traditional IRA, the penalty may not apply to part or all of the distributions that comes out of contributions.

The Timely Contribution Withdrawal

If an IRA investor makes a contribution to a *traditional* IRA for a given year, doesn't take a deduction for it and then withdraws the contribution before the due date (including extensions) of his or her income tax return for that year, the IRS will *not* consider the withdrawal of the contribution to be a "taxable distribution."

However, any interest or other income earned on the contribution—which also must be withdrawn—is treated as reportable income in the year in which the contribution was made. This withdrawn interest or other income may be subject to the 10 percent additional tax on early withdrawals.

■ RETIREMENT DISTRIBUTIONS

Roth IRA investors are not taxed on retirement distributions taken after age 59½ if the IRA was held for five years. Before the five-year holding period is met, withdrawals come from contributions first and are tax free. Withdrawals from earnings are taxed as ordinary income.

Traditional IRA investors must report IRA distributions in their gross incomes in the year when the distributions are received. Exceptions to this general rule include rollovers, timely withdrawals of contributions and the return of nondeductible contributions.

Traditional IRA distributions are taxed as ordinary income. Special averaging (that is, five-year or ten-year forward averaging) that is available for lump-sum distributions from qualified employer-sponsored retirement plans is not available with IRA distributions. Also, IRA distributions are not treated as capital gains.

Fully or Partially Taxable Distributions

An individual's traditional IRA distribution may be fully or partially taxable, depending on whether his or her IRA includes only deductible contributions or any nondeductible contributions.

If only deductible contributions were made to a person's traditional IRA (or IRAs, if he or she has more than one) at any time, then he or she has no "basis" in the IRA. Because the person has no basis in the IRA, all distributions are fully taxable in the year when they are received.

If a traditional IRA investor made nondeductible contributions to any of his or her IRAs, figuring tax liability becomes more complicated. The IRA owner has a cost basis (after-tax investment in the IRA) to the extent of the nondeductible contributions. Such nondeductible contributions are *not* taxed when they are distributed from the IRA. They are considered to be a return of the owner's after-tax invested capital.

When traditional IRA distributions are paid, special rules must be followed to compute the tax on the distributions if:

- only nondeductible contributions were made and there have been earnings or gains; or

- if both deductible and nondeductible contributions were made.

Only the part of the distribution that represents the IRA owner's cost basis (the nondeductible contributions) is tax free. For IRAs that contain nondeductible contributions, distributions will be considered to consist partly of nondeductible contributions (basis) and partly of deductible contributions, earnings or gains. Thus, until a taxpayer fully recovers his or her basis in the IRA, each distribution is partly taxable and partly nontaxable.

To figure the taxable and nontaxable portions of a traditional IRA distribution, there is a three-step procedure:

1. Figure the percentage of the account balance (prior to the distribution) that came from nondeductible contributions.

2. Multiply the total distribution by the percentage you calculated in Step 1. This is the nontaxable portion of the distribution.

3. Subtract the nontaxable portion from the total distribution. This is the taxable portion.

Illustration 4.3 shows how this works. (In practice, however, IRA owners should use Form 8606.)

Form 8606

An individual is required to complete Form 8606 if he or she received an IRA distribution and, at any time, made nondeductible IRA contributions. The individual may use the form to figure the nontaxable distributions for a given tax year and the total IRA basis for the current and earlier years. This form must be attached to the regular income tax Form 1040.

ILL. 4.3 ■ *Figuring Taxable and Nontaxable Portions of an IRA Distribution*

Over the years, Karen made the following contributions to her IRAs:

Year	Deductible Contribution	Nondeductible Contribution
1991	$2,000	$0
1992	2,000	0
1993	2,000	0
1994	1,000	0
1995	1,000	0
1996	700	300
1997	700	300
Total	$9,400	$600

Though she stopped making contributions to her accounts after 1997, thanks to earnings, Karen's IRAs continue to grow. As of December 31, 2001, her funds are valued at $25,000. At the beginning of 2002, she takes her first distribution, which is $5,000. If Karen did not have any basis in her IRAs, the full $5,000 would be taxable. However, given that she has a $600 cost basis in her plans, a portion of that $5,000 distribution will be received tax free. Here is how Karen would calculate the taxable and nontaxable portions of this distribution:

Value of IRA(s) as of December 31, 2001:	$25,000
Karen's total IRA cost basis:	$600
Step 1: Cost basis as a % of total IRA value ($600 ÷ $25,000):	2.4%
Step 2: Nontaxable portion of the distribution ($5,000 × .024):	$120
Step 3: Taxable portion of the distribution ($5,000 − $120):	$4,880

Karen's cost basis in her IRAs is now reduced by $120 to $480. She would continue to follow the above steps, adjusting the percentage of cost basis for each year a distribution is taken, until she recovers her full $600 cost basis. From that point on, all distributions would be fully taxable.

Contributions and Distributions in the Same Year

In many cases, it's not unusual for an IRA owner to take a distribution in the same year he or she makes a contribution. If an IRA owner makes an IRA contribution that may be nondeductible because he or she is covered by an employer retirement plan, the IRA owner also needs to use a special worksheet. The worksheet helps the IRA owner determine the amount that must be included in income for any part of the IRA distribution that represents deductible contributions, earnings or gains. If the IRA owner has more than one IRA, he or she must consider the distributions together as if they were a single IRA.

If an IRA owner is, in fact, covered by an employer plan and has made IRA contributions for the current year that may be deductible, the worksheet shown in Ill. 4.4 can be used to determine how much of his or her current year IRA distribution is tax free and how much is taxable.

Recognizing Losses on IRA Investments

If an IRA investor has a loss on his or her IRA investment, then he or she can recognize the loss on his or her income tax return, but only when all the amounts in all of his or her IRA accounts have been distributed and the total distributions are less than his or her unrecovered basis—the total amount of the nondeductible contributions in a traditional IRA or any contributions to a Roth IRA. He or she can claim the loss as a miscellaneous itemized deduction as long as the total of miscellaneous itemized deductions exceeds 2 percent of adjusted gross income.

For example, Brian has made nondeductible contributions to a traditional IRA totaling $2,000, giving him a basis of $2,000 at the end of 1997. By the end of 1998, his IRA earned $400 of interest income. In that year, Brian withdrew $600, reducing the value of his IRA to $1,800 at year's end. Using Form 8606 to help him with his

---

ILL. 4.4 ■ *Worksheet: Taxable Portion of IRA Distribution*

1. Enter the basis in all IRA(s) as of December 31, last year. $_____

2. Enter all IRA contributions made for this year, regardless of whether they are deductible. (Contributions to be made from January 1 through April 15 of next year should be included; however, do not include contributions rolled over from retirement plans.) $_____

3. Add lines 1 and 2. $_____

4. Enter the value of all IRA(s) as of December 31 of this year (include any outstanding rollovers). $_____

5. Enter the total IRA distributions received this year (do not include outstanding rollovers). $_____

6. Add lines 4 and 5. $_____

7. Divide line 3 by line 6. Enter the result as a decimal (to at least two places), but do not enter more than 1.00. $_____

8. Nontaxable portion of the distribution (multiply line 5 by line 7). $_____

9. Taxable portion of the distribution (subtract line 8 from line 5). $_____

calculations, Brian determines the taxable part of the distribution and his remaining basis.

In 1999, Brian's IRA had a *loss* of $500. At the end of that year, Brian's IRA balance was $1,300. Brian's remaining basis in his IRA is $1,500. Brian withdrew the $1,300 balance remaining in the IRA. He can claim a loss for 1999 of $200 (the $1,300 withdrawn less the remaining $1,500 cost basis).

Distribution in the Form of an Annuity

An IRA owner may tell his or her IRA custodian to use the amount in the account to buy an annuity contract. If the IRA is a Roth IRA and the account was held for five years, the annuity is tax free.

If the IRA is a traditional IRA and only deductible contributions were made to the IRA since it was set up, the annuity payments are fully taxable. If an owner's IRA includes both deductible and nondeductible contributions, the annuity payments will be partially taxable. Amounts corresponding to the owner's basis will be excluded from tax liability because the owner has already paid taxes on that money.

The calculation used to compute the taxable portion of an annuity is similar to the one used to compute the taxable portion of a single payment, but the ratio is computed in a way that takes into account the fact that the withdrawals are taken over many years. In most cases, the withdrawals are taken over the life of the IRA owner or the joint lives of the owner and a beneficiary. Illustration 4.5 shows how this works.

■ INHERITED IRAs

The beneficiaries of participants' Roth IRAs may withdraw funds from the IRA if the account had been held for five years or they may wait until the five-year period passes. Withdrawals before that date are tax free if taken from contributions and taxed if taken from earnings (just as the investor could if still alive).

The beneficiaries of participants' traditional IRAs must include distributions to them in their gross incomes. Beneficiaries can be virtually anyone the IRA owner chooses. A spousal beneficiary can elect to treat the entire inherited interest as his or her own IRA.

A nonspousal beneficiary may not treat an inherited IRA as though the beneficiary established it. The IRA cannot be combined with another IRA. No deduction will be permitted for amounts deposited into an inherited IRA. Also, nondeductible contributions cannot be made into an IRA that is inherited by a nonspousal beneficiary.

If an individual inherits an IRA from a deceased owner who had a basis in the IRA due to nondeductible contributions, then that basis remains with the IRA and it transfers to the beneficiary. However, beneficiaries may not claim a death benefit exclusion (as is available with certain distributions from qualified plans) for any part of the distribution from an inherited IRA.

ILL. 4.5 ■ *Figuring Taxable and Nontaxable Portions of Annuity Distributions*

Molly's traditional IRA is valued at $48,000 and $15,000 of it came in the form of nondeductible contributions. At her direction, the custodian of the IRA purchases an annuity that will pay her $5,500 per year for 20 years.

Based on the annuity provider's guarantee, Molly will receive a total of $110,000 over the life of the annuity.

Instead of comparing the nondeductible contributions to the account value, as we did in Step 1 of the single payment calculation, we compare it to the total amount Molly expects to receive under the annuity contract. The calculation gives you the nontaxable percentage for an annuity, which is called the "exclusion ratio."

The exclusion ratio for an IRA is equal to the sum of the nondeductible contributions divided by the sum of the annuity payments that are expected. Based on these facts, Molly's exclusion ratio is computed as follows:

Step 1: Exclusion ratio ($15,000 ÷ $110,000): 13.64%

(The remainder of the calculation is similar to Steps 2 and 3 used for a single payment withdrawal.)

Step 2: Nontaxable portion of the distribution ($5,500 × 13.64%): $750

Step 3: Taxable portion of the distribution ($5,500 − $750): $4,750

Most IRA annuities are not term-certain annuities like Molly's (hers was a term of 20 years). Most are annuities for the life of the investor (or the joint lives of the investor and his or her beneficiaries). The calculation of the exclusion ratio is the same as you've just done, but you use an IRA "life expectancy" instead of the fixed term. (The IRS tables of life expectancies appear later on in this chapter in Ill. 4.7 and Ill. 4.8.) If Molly had purchased a life annuity at age 65, her calculation would be the same to the penny, because her life expectancy at that age is set by the IRS at 20 years.

IRAs and the Federal Estate Tax

Beneficiaries of participants' IRAs may be able to claim a federal estate tax deduction for certain distributions from a decedent's IRA. If a beneficiary receives a lump-sum distribution from an IRA, the IRS taxes it as "income in respect to the decedent" to the extent of net IRA balance. (This refers to the balance as of the date of death minus the IRA owner's basis.)

Because the IRS generally adheres to the notion that distributions should face federal taxation only once, when the beneficiary reports income in respect to a decedent, he or she can deduct the part of federal estate tax that corresponds to that income.

Reporting and Withholding Requirements

A custodian is required to withhold federal income tax from IRA distributions unless the owner chooses not to have tax withheld. When IRA owners receive a distribution from their IRAs, they will be sent Form 1099-R—"Distributions from Pensions, Annuities, Retirement or Profit-Sharing Plans, IRAs, Insurance Contracts, etc."

The tax withheld from an annuity or a similar payment is based on the owner's marital status and the number of exemptions claimed on a "withholding certificate" (Form W-4P). A taxpayer who does not file a certificate will be treated for withholding purposes as a married individual claiming three withholding allowances.

For the most part, custodians will withhold 10 percent on lump-sum distributions. Special rules apply for U.S citizens living outside the United States.

Reporting Taxable Distributions

IRA owners who receive taxable distributions from their IRAs, including premature distributions, will report them on the appropriate lines of their Form 1040 or 1040As. They cannot be reported on the more simplified Form 1040EZ (see Ill. 4.6).

■ REQUIRED DISTRIBUTIONS

Funds must come out of an IRA eventually and the IRS does not leave the matter to chance. But the requirements for withdrawing IRA funds vary, depending on

---

ILL. 4.6 ■ *Part of Form 1040 (Line 15a)*

Income

Attach Copy B of your Forms W-2, W-2G, and 1099-R here.

If you did not get a W-2, see page 12.

Enclose but do not attach any payment. Also, please use Form 1040-V.

7	Wages, salaries, tips, etc. Attach Form(s) W-2	7	
8a	**Taxable** interest. Attach Schedule B if required	8a	
b	**Tax-exempt** interest. DO NOT include on line 8a. **8b**		
9	Dividends. Attach Schedule B if required	9	
10	Taxable refunds, credits, or offsets of state and local income taxes (see page 12)	10	
11	Alimony received	11	
12	Business income or (loss). Attach Schedule C or C-EZ	12	
13	Capital gain or (loss). Attach Schedule D	13	
14	Other gains or (losses). Attach Form 4797	14	
15a	Total IRA distributions . **15a** **b** Taxable amount (see page 13)	15b	
16a	Total pensions and annuities **16a** **b** Taxable amount (see page 13)	16b	
17	Rental real estate, royalties, partnerships, S corporations, trusts, etc. Attach Schedule E	17	
18	Farm income or (loss). Attach Schedule F	18	
19	Unemployment compensation	19	
20a	Social security benefits . **20a** **b** Taxable amount (see page 14)	20b	
21	Other income. List type and amount—see page 15	21	
22	Add the amounts in the far right column for lines 7 through 21. This is your **total income** ▶	22	

whether the party making the withdrawal is the actual IRA investor or the beneficiary of a decedent's IRA.

The owner of a Roth IRA is not required to ever make any withdrawals. He or she may keep funds in the account until death. A traditional IRA investor, however, must withdraw the balance in his or her IRA in one of two ways:

1. by starting to withdraw *periodic distributions* of the balance in the IRA by the required beginning date; or

2. by withdrawing the *entire balance* in the IRA by the required beginning date.

Age 70½ Rule—for Traditional IRAs Only

The IRS has established a definite date for beginning distribution from a traditional IRA. This requirement is known as the "required beginning date" (RBD) or the "age 70½ rule."

According to this rule, if traditional IRA distributions did not start earlier, they must start on or before April 1 of the year following the calendar year when an IRA owner becomes age 70½. Although this first distribution isn't required to be made until April 1 of the year *after* the year in which the traditional IRA investor reaches age 70½, the distribution actually counts *for* the year in which the owner indeed becomes 70½.

The initial required distribution is the only one that may be delayed in this way. The required minimum distribution for any year *after* the traditional IRA owner's 70½ year must be made no later than December 31 of that later year.

If an IRA owner elects to defer receipt of the first required distribution until the year after he or she turns 70½, then there will be the equivalent of two distributions received that year: the one that applies to the previous (age 70½) year and the one that is required for the current year. And, of course, the recipient will be taxed on both distributions in that year.

Sounds complicated? Then consider this example: Bob Martin, who has not yet taken any distributions from his traditional IRA, turns 70½ in 1998. His *initial* required distribution applies to 1998—although he does not have to actually take the distribution until April 1, 1999. The *second* required distribution is applicable to 1999 and must be distributed no later than December 31, 1999. If Bob receives the first distribution in early 1999, he will need to report and owe tax on the first two required distributions in 1999.

■ IRA MINIMUM DISTRIBUTION REQUIREMENTS

Because the investment appreciation and some contributions to an IRA have not previously been taxed, the IRS's *minimum distribution requirements* prevent IRA owners from distributing the account balance(s) over a long period of time. In short, the minimum distribution requirements were established to limit the maximum period over which IRA distributions may be spread.

To comply with this requirement, minimum distributions from IRAs must begin no later than the "required beginning date" (RBD) and must be based on one or a combination of the following payout schedules:

- the life of the owner;

- the lives of the owner and the beneficiary;

- a period certain not extending beyond the life expectancy of the owner; or

- a period certain not extending beyond the joint-life expectancy of the owner and the beneficiary.

If an IRA owner has more than one beneficiary and all are individuals (rather than charities or foundations), the beneficiary with the *shortest* life expectancy will be the designated beneficiary used to determine the period over which withdrawals must be made. (According to the IRS, a *designated beneficiary* means any individual named by the IRA owner to receive his or her IRA balance upon the owner's death.)

As of the required beginning date, IRA balances are required to make minimum distributions each year based on the life expectancy of the owner or joint-life expectancy of the owner and beneficiary, if applicable. If a particular lifetime distribution option is chosen under which payments start before the RBD, perhaps at age 65, those payments do not fall under the minimum distribution rules, but payments after RBD must meet the rules.

Failure to satisfy the minimum distribution requirements can result in a nondeductible *50 percent penalty tax* on the difference between the amount that should have been distributed and the amount that was actually distributed.

Thus, if the minimum distribution requirement for a given year was $5,000, but the actual distribution is only $3,000, the $2,000 shortfall will be subject to the 50 percent penalty tax. This penalty is in addition to the income tax payable on the full minimum distribution. The penalty tax is calculated as follows:

$5,000	Required minimum distribution
−3,000	Amount actually distributed
$2,000	Excess accumulation
× .50	Penalty tax
$1,000	Penalty owing

Penalty Waiver

The IRS is anxious to assure that minimum distributions are taken in a timely manner. However, the IRS doesn't want to penalize IRA owners who fail to take minimum distributions due to a "reasonable error." The IRS considers that a reasonable error may have occurred if the IRA owner:

- took incorrect advice from a plan administrator or consultant;

- incorrectly calculated the minimum distribution himself or herself; or

- misunderstood how the proper amount was to be calculated.

In cases of reasonable error, the IRS may waive the penalty after the IRA owner completes several steps. The IRA owner must first pay the penalty and then request a waiver. The waiver request is attached to his or her income tax form. If the waiver is granted, the IRS will refund the penalty paid.

Owner Dies After Required Distributions Start

If periodic distributions that satisfy the IRS's minimum requirements have started and the IRA owner dies, any undistributed amounts at the owner's death must be paid out at least as rapidly as under the distribution method being used at the owner's death.

There is one exception to this rule: If the beneficiary is the owner's surviving spouse who elects to treat the IRA as his or her own, then the surviving spouse is considered to be the "new" owner. He or she is then subject to the same rules for required minimum distributions that normally apply to IRA owners.

Owner Dies Before Required Distributions Start

If the IRA owner dies before his or her RBD and before any distributions that satisfy the minimum distribution requirement have begun, the *entire interest* in the IRA must be distributed under one of the following choices:

- **Choice 1**. By December 31 of the *fifth* year following the owner's death.

- **Choice 2**. Over the life of the designated beneficiary or over a period not extending beyond the life expectancy of the designated beneficiary. Distributions must begin by December 31 of the year following the year of the owner's death.

In most cases, the IRA owner (or beneficiary) may predetermine (and build into the IRA documents) which choice applies. If the beneficiary makes the decision, then the decision must be made no later than December 31 of the year following the year the IRA owner died.

If no distribution decision is made, distributions must be made over the life or life expectancy of the designated beneficiary (Choice 2) if the beneficiary is the surviving spouse (which is often the case). This assumes that the spouse did not elect to treat the IRA as his or her own. If the beneficiary is *not* the surviving spouse, the IRA must be distributed by December 31 of the fifth year following the year of the owner's death (Choice 1).

As the beneficiary of a deceased spouse's IRA, the surviving spouse may decide not to treat the IRA as his or her own and instead elect an extended distribution (under Choice 2). In this case, distribution must begin no later than December 31 of the year the IRA owner (now deceased) would have reached 70½.

Calculating Minimum Distributions

The owner of an IRA is required to figure the minimum amount that must be distributed from his or her IRA each year (the "required minimum distribution," or RMD). Special rules apply if the IRA is an individual retirement annuity.

The required minimum distribution from an IRA can be determined by dividing the total of all IRA account values as of December 31 of the preceding year by the applicable life expectancy provided on tables supplied by the IRS.

The *applicable life expectancy* is:

- the IRA owner's remaining (single) life expectancy;

- the remaining joint-life expectancy of the IRA owner and his or her designated beneficiary; or

- the remaining life expectancy of the designated beneficiary (if the IRA owner dies before distributions have begun).

Unless the IRA owner refigures his (or his spouse's) life expectancy each year, the life expectancy must be reduced by one for each year that has elapsed since the date life expectancy was first determined.

Determining Life Expectancy

Life expectancies, for the purposes of the IRS, are determined from life expectancy tables, such as Table I, shown in Ill. 4.7, and Table II, shown in Ill. 4.8. To determine one's annual minimum distribution, a person must use the correct table. Table I is appropriate if the periodic payments are for the IRA owner's life only. Table II should be used if payments are for the lives of both the IRA owner and his or her beneficiary.

For distributions that start by the required beginning date, life expectancies should be determined using the ages of the owner and the beneficiary as of their birthdays in the IRA owner's 70½ year. If the owner dies before distributions have begun, the designated beneficiary's life expectancy is determined from Table I using the beneficiary's age based on his or her birthday in the year that distributions must begin.

Let's say that 70-year-old Ed has an IRA and must take a minimum distribution. The value of the IRA as of December 31 last year was $250,000. If he chose to take distributions over his single life expectancy, the amount due for this year would be $15,625 ($250,000 divided by 16.0). If he chose to take distributions over the joint-life expectancy of himself and his 66-year-old wife, Clara, the minimum due this year would be $11,111 ($250,000 divided by 22.5).

ILL. 4.7 ■ *Table I: IRS Life Expectancy Table for Single Life*

Age	Life Expectancy	Age	Life Expectancy
56	27.7	76	11.9
57	26.8	77	11.2
58	25.9	78	10.6
59	25.0	79	10.0
60	24.2	80	9.5
61	23.3	81	8.9
62	22.5	82	8.4
63	21.6	83	7.9
64	20.8	84	7.4
65	20.0	85	6.9
66	19.2	86	6.5
67	18.4	87	6.1
68	17.6	88	5.7
69	16.8	89	5.3
70	16.0	90	5.0
71	15.3	91	4.7
72	14.6	92	4.4
73	13.9	93	4.1
74	13.2	94	3.9
75	12.5		

Complete Table I can be found in Appendix E of IRS Publication 590.

Recalculating Life Expectancy

Most IRA plan documents require that the life of the IRA owner (and his or her spouse, if the spouse is designated as joint beneficiary) must be *refigured* each year when calculating the required minimum distribution due. *Refiguring life expectancy* simply means returning to the appropriate IRS life expectancy table—single or joint life, whichever was elected for RMD purposes—and using the owner's (and spouse's, if applicable) *actual* age according to his or her birthday (and the spouse's birthday) during the specific tax year to determine the applicable life expectancy divisor.

For example, let's return to Ed and Clara and assume Ed elected a joint-life payout period for his required distributions. For the first distribution, when Ed is 70 and Clara is 66, the joint period is 22.5 years. (See Ill. 4.8.) If they were to refigure life expectancy, they would return to Table II in the second year to determine a new joint-life period based on their attained ages—Ed is now 71 and Clara is 67. A refigured joint-life expectancy for year two is 21.7 years. This would be the divisor used to calculate the RMD for the second year. The third year it would be 20.8, and so on.

On the other hand, if the IRA owner elects not to refigure life expectancy, he or she simply subtracts one (1) from the first and subsequent life expectancy periods. Continuing with our example, if Ed elected not to refigure the couple's joint-life expectancy, the divisor for year two would be 21.5, for year three it would be 20.5, and so on.

ILL. 4.8 ■ *Table II: IRS Life Expectancy Table for Joint Lives*

Participant's Age	Beneficiary's Age													
	55	56	57	58	59	60	61	62	63	64	65	66	67	68
70	29.9	29.1	28.4	27.6	26.9	26.2	25.6	24.9	24.3	23.7	23.1	22.5	22.0	21.5
71	29.7	29.0	28.2	27.5	26.7	26.0	25.3	24.7	24.0	23.4	22.8	22.2	21.7	21.2
72	29.6	28.8	28.1	27.3	26.5	25.8	25.1	24.4	23.8	23.1	22.5	21.9	21.3	20.8
73	29.5	28.7	27.9	27.1	26.4	25.6	24.9	24.2	23.5	22.9	22.2	21.6	21.0	20.5
74	29.4	28.6	27.8	27.0	26.2	25.5	24.7	24.0	23.3	22.7	22.0	21.4	20.8	20.2
75	29.3	28.5	27.7	26.9	26.1	25.3	24.6	23.8	23.1	22.4	21.8	21.1	20.5	19.9

Complete Table II can be found in Appendix E of IRS Publication 590.

There are a number of important points to note about refiguring life expectancy:

1. The election to refigure or not refigure must be made by the date the first required minimum distribution is due.

2. If a joint-life expectancy is refigured annually and either the IRA owner or the spouse dies, then the survivor's life is used to calculate minimum distributions for the years after the death occurred.

3. If life expectancies are refigured each year and the IRA owner dies and then the spouse dies after the required distribution date, the entire value of the IRA must be distributed before the last day of the year after the surviving spouse's death.

4. Although the life of the IRA owner may always be refigured, for beneficiaries, only spouses' lives may be refigured. If the IRA beneficiary is not the spouse and a joint-life election is made and the owner elects to refigure his or her own life, then an additional calculation must be performed to determine the appropriate RMD for any given year. This calculation is the same as that used for the minimum distribution incidental benefit (MDIB) requirement, which is explained below.

Minimum Distribution Incidental Benefit

Distributions from an IRA during the owner's lifetime must meet the *minimum distribution incidental benefit*, or MDIB, requirement. The MDIB requirement basically says that when calculating the joint-life expectancy of an IRA owner and a nonspousal beneficiary, the difference in ages cannot exceed 10 years. The IRS imposes this requirement to ensure that IRAs are used mainly to provide retirement benefits for their owners. After the IRA owner's death, only "incidental" benefits are expected to stay in the IRA to be paid out to the beneficiary. Essentially, this requirement lessens the advantage to naming a very young person as a joint-life beneficiary of one's IRA.

ILL. 4.9 ■ *Tables for Applicable Divisors for MDIB**

Age	Applicable Divisor	Age	Applicable Divisor
70	26.2	93	8.8
71	25.3	94	8.3
72	24.4	95	7.8
73	23.5	96	7.3
74	22.7	97	6.9
75	21.8	98	6.5
76	20.9	99	6.1
77	20.1	100	5.7
78	19.2	101	5.3
79	18.4	102	5.0
80	17.6	103	4.7
81	16.8	104	4.4
82	16.0	105	4.1
83	15.3	106	3.8
84	14.5	107	3.6
85	13.8	108	3.3
86	13.1	109	3.1
87	12.4	110	2.8
88	11.8	111	2.6
89	11.1	112	2.4
90	10.5	113	2.2
91	9.9	114	2.0
92	9.4	115+	1.8

*Minimum Distribution Incidental Benefit

To calculate a required minimum distribution that also satisfies the MDIB rules, the IRA owner must complete the following steps. As you can see, these steps are for the RMD in year one and for the RMD in subsequent years.

MDIB Requirement for Year One RMD

Step 1. Using the "Table for Determining Applicable Divisor for MDIB" (Ill. 4.9), find the applicable divisor for the IRA owner's age. The IRA owner should use the age that corresponds to his or her birthday in the year for which the distribution is being figured.

Step 2. The IRA owner compares the MDIB divisor against the joint-life expectancy period from Table II (Ill. 4.8). The *smaller* of these two is used to calculate the RMD in the first year. (Note: In cases where the nonspousal beneficiary is more than 10 years younger than the IRA owner, the MDIB divisor will always be smaller and thus, will always be the one used.)

Step 3. The RMD for year one is calculated by dividing the total amount in the owner's IRAs as of December 31 of the preceding year by the (smaller) number in Step 2.

For example, let's say Oliver, born October 1, 1927, became 70½ in 1998. The value of his sole IRA as of December 31, 1997, was $58,000. Oliver's IRA beneficiary is his brother Sam, who turned 56 in 1998. Oliver knows that he has to take a minimum distribution from his IRA for 1998. He elects to have his required distributions based on the joint-life expectancy of himself and his brother. He also elects to refigure his own life expectancy; his brother's cannot be refigured. For the RMD for 1998, Oliver must use the divisor in the MDIB table (Ill. 4.9), since his beneficiary is more than 10 years younger than he is. Thus, Oliver's required distribution for 1998 is $2,292 ($58,000 divided by 25.3). Assuming no other withdrawals, his adjusted 1998 account balance, which will be used for calculating his 1999 distribution, is $55,708. (For purposes of this example, interest earnings on the declining IRA balance have been ignored.)

MDIB Requirement for Year Two (and Beyond) RMD

Now let's move ahead. It's one year later and time again for Oliver to take the required distribution from his IRA. That will be his adjusted IRA balance as of December 31, 1998, or $55,708, divided by his and Sam's joint-life expectancy. Remember, Oliver elected to refigure his own life, but cannot refigure his brother's life. The joint-life expectancy for year two is calculated as follows:

Step 1	Life expectancy of the beneficiary, using his age as of his birthday in the first distribution year (i.e., in 1998), based on single life expectancy table (Ill. 4.7):	27.7
Step 2	Number of years that have passed since first distribution year:	1.0
Step 3	Remaining life expectancy of beneficiary (Step 1 minus Step 2):	26.7
Step 4	Divisor in Table I (Ill. 4.7) that is closest to but less than the amount in Step 3. Enter the age shown for that divisor amount:	58
Step 5	IRA owner's age as of his or her birthday this year:	72
Step 6	Joint-life expectancy of ages in Step 4 and Step 5, using Table II (Ill. 4.8):	27.3
Step 7	Applicable divisor from MDIB table (Ill. 4.9), based on owner's age in Step 5:	24.4
Step 8	Refigured life expectancy (using *smaller* of Step 6 and Step 7):	24.4

Oliver's required minimum distribution for 1999, using the refigured life expectancy, is $2,283 ($55,708 divided by 24.4).

The MDIB requirement doesn't apply to distributions paid in years after the death of an original IRA account owner. Consequently, if an individual holds an IRA as a beneficiary of a deceased IRA owner, minimum distributions from the IRA can be calculated using the general rules for distributions.

Miscellaneous Rules for Minimum Distributions

The yearly minimum distribution can be taken however the owner desires (all at once or periodically, such as monthly or quarterly) as long as the total distributions for the year equal the required minimum amount. Remember, an IRA owner can always take *more* than the required minimum.

If an individual has more than one IRA, he or she must determine the minimum distribution separately for each IRA. However, the owner may total the minimum amounts from all IRAs and take the total from any one or more of the IRA accounts.

For example, Harry Penworthy is 72 and his wife is 66. He has two IRAs. Harry's account balance in IRA A is $10,000; his account balance in IRA B is $20,000. Harry elects a single life payout for IRA A ($10,000 divided by 14.6, the single life expectancy as shown in Ill. 4.7) and a joint-life payout for IRA B ($20,000 divided by 21.9, the joint-life expectancy of Harry and his wife as shown in Ill. 4.8). The total required distribution that must be taken from Harry's IRAs is $1,598 ($685 plus $913). Harry can take $1,598 from IRA A or IRA B, or he can take distributions from both IRAs as long as they total $1,598.

If an individual takes more in any year than the required minimum amount for that year, he or she will not receive credit for the additional amount when figuring the minimum distribution amounts for future years. The exception to this involves required distributions in the 70½ year. Any amount distributed in the 70½ year will be credited toward the amount that must be distributed no later than April 1 of the following year.

■ SUMMARY

As time goes on and more people with IRAs and SEPs reach their retirement years, there will be growing concern about the rules and procedures for distributing the IRA money. The IRS insists that taxpayers begin withdrawals from their IRAs by certain dates.

From age 59½, IRA owners no longer have to pay the 10 percent penalty tax for taking money out of an IRA. Between ages 59½ and 70½, IRA owners have the greatest flexibility in taking distributions from their IRAs. Within this age window, an IRA owner can pay himself or herself as much or as little as he or she likes, although most distributions will be taxable.

Inherited IRAs also have to be distributed. However, a beneficiary, who is also the spouse of the deceased owner, may choose to treat the IRA as his or her own and then wait many years before making distributions from the inherited IRA.

■ **CHAPTER 4 QUESTIONS FOR REVIEW**

1. A 10 percent penalty applies to taxable withdrawals from a Roth IRA under which of the following circumstances?

   A. The IRA owner becomes disabled.

   B. The IRA owner dies.

   C. The IRA owner receives an annuity-type distribution.

   D. The IRA owner becomes unemployed.

2. A traditional IRA owner can meet the minimum distribution requirement by

   A. starting to withdraw periodic distributions of the balance in the IRA by the required beginning date

   B. withdrawing the entire balance in the IRA by the required beginning date

   C. either A and B

   D. neither A nor B

3. The required beginning date for distributions from a Roth IRA is

   A. the IRA owner's 59½ birthday

   B. the IRA owner's 70½ birthday

   C. April 1 of the year following the year in which the IRA owner becomes 70½

   D. There is no required beginning date.

4. The required beginning date for distributions from a traditional IRA is

   A. the IRA owner's 59½ birthday

   B. the IRA owner's 70½ birthday

   C. April 1 of the year following the year in which the IRA owner become 70½

   D. There is no required beginning date.

5. If the minimum distribution requirement for a given year was $4,000, but the actual IRA distribution is only $3,000, the penalty is

   A. $250

   B. $500

   C. $1,000

   D. $2,000

5

Rollovers, Transfers and Conversions

T he Internal Revenue Service has long allowed tax-free rollovers or transfers of cash or other assets from one retirement program to another to preserve the special tax-deferred status of retirement accounts. People make rollovers for convenience, to obtain a better return on investments or simply because they are unhappy with the party handling their account and want to switch to a new custodian.

The introduction of Roth IRAs introduced a new use for a rollover: the conversion of a traditional IRA into a Roth. A conversion rollover is not tax free, however, because the two types of IRA are fundamentally different. With a traditional IRA, the tax is paid when money is withdrawn. With a Roth IRA, tax is paid before a contribution is made (that is, contributions are not tax deductible) and then never again (if all requirements are met).

The IRS does not allow an investor to convert a traditional IRA into a Roth IRA unless the tax is paid—for the year of the rollover. A special rule applies for 1998 conversions that allow the tax to be spread over four years.

Properly handled, rollovers preserve tax benefits for the investor. Handled improperly, the IRS rejects the rollover, and the participant faces possible penalties and loss of the special tax status.

This chapter examines the various types of rollovers available and then looks at the IRS rules that govern rollovers and transfers.

■ ■ ■ ■ ■

■ DIFFERENCES BETWEEN ROLLOVERS AND TRANSFERS

The terms *rollover* and *transfer* are typically used to describe any movement of funds from a qualified plan or an IRA to another IRA investment (including Roth IRAs). There are, however, important differences between a rollover and a transfer.

IRA funds are *rolled over* when a client's retirement plan is liquidated and a check is sent by the trustee directly to the client. This would apply when a lump-sum distribution is received from a qualified plan or the money is withdrawn from a previously established IRA.

In a rollover, the investor has 60 days to reinvest in another IRA (from the time the money is received) without paying current taxes on the rollover amount. If he or she does not reinvest the money within 60 days, the amount is subject to tax and possibly a 10 percent penalty. Only one rollover is allowed per year, per IRA. Thus, if an individual has five IRA accounts, he or she can roll over each account once a year.

An IRA, however, is *transferred* when the money is sent directly by one financial institution to another, bypassing the owner entirely. There are no legal restrictions on the number of times a transfer can take place in a given year. Some custodians, though, may impose restrictions on how many transfers will be permitted in one year and may even impose fees on each transfer. Therefore, the IRA owner should investigate possible restrictions and costs before transferring IRA funds.

■ TYPES OF ROLLOVERS

Rollovers come in three types: (1) traditional IRA to Roth IRA (the conversion rollover), (2) IRA to another IRA of the same type and (2) qualified employee plan to a traditional IRA. Roth IRAs may not accept rollovers from qualified employee plans.

Rollovers from Traditional IRA to Roth IRA—The Conversion

A rollover from a traditional IRA to a Roth IRA is not tax free. An investor who converts to a Roth IRA must pay regular income tax (no penalty) on the entire rollover amount *minus* any nondeductible contributions that had ever been made to the traditional IRA being rolled over. If the rollover takes place in 1998, this tax is spread over four years. Otherwise, it is paid in the year the rollover occurs.

So why would someone do this? As strange as it may seem, the choice is economically the same as deciding where to put new IRA contributions—even though the price of making the conversion is paying tax now. That's really the same choice an investor makes when opening a new Roth IRA.

The hope is that permanent tax exemption of the Roth IRA is worth more than the immediate tax that must be paid on the conversion rollover. Often, this will be the case—but, of course, the investor has to come up with cash from other sources. Taking the tax money out of the rollover is possible, but the amount *not* rolled over is subject to the 10 percent penalty if the investor is under the age of 59½.

Just as regular contributions to Roth IRAs are restricted to investors of low and middle income, conversion rollovers are similarly restricted. No conversion rollover is permitted if the investor's adjusted gross income for the year of the rollover exceeds $100,000 or if the investor is married and files his or her tax return separately.

ILL. 5.1 ■ *Converting to a Roth IRA—A Case Study*

Joan Cummings has an IRA worth $100,000. Should she convert it into a Roth?

Scenario 1—Rollover Is Better

Cummings is in the 28 percent tax bracket and expects to be in the same bracket in 20 years when she retires. Whether she converts the account or not, the balance in 20 years at 10 percent will be $672,750. The question is whether it is better to pay the tax on $100,000 now or on $672,750 in 20 years. In other words, would it be better to pay $28,000 now or $188,370 in 20 years?

The answer is: It would be better to pay the $28,000 now, if Cummings has it. In other words, Cummings should convert to a Roth IRA.

How is this conclusion reached? The only way to compare is to see what would happen if Cummings held on to her traditional IRA and invested $28,000 (the amount she would have to pay for the conversion rollover) in a *taxable* account for the same 20 years at the same 10 percent rate. If she does this, she'll have $112,474 in the separate account, which will fall short of the $188,370 tax bill she'll get on the traditional IRA. So, with the Roth IRA, she ends up with $672,750, but with the traditional IRA she ends up with $596,854 ($672,750 minus the taxes not covered by the separate taxable account).

Scenario 2—Rollover Is Worse Than Keeping Traditional IRA

Let's say Cummings expects her retirement income to be lower than her current income and that would put her in the 15 percent bracket when she retires. The big cost of a traditional IRA is the tax at retirement. With a lower retirement cost, the conclusion reverses.

Instead of paying $188,370 in tax at retirement on her traditional IRA, Cummings now expects the tax at retirement to be $100,912. Cummings's separate taxable account (remember the $28,000 she set aside?) grows to $112,474 and now covers the tax, leaving an extra $11,562 if she just holds on to the traditional IRA.

Scenario 3—It's a Close Call

Let's say that Cummings makes the projections found in Scenario 2: 28 percent bracket now and an anticipated 15 percent bracket in 20 years. But she likes some of the features of the Roth IRA—the ability to withdraw contributions for any reason, if she needs to, for example. Is there a way to convert without losing the $11,562 she figured in the last scenario?

Yes. If she makes the conversion rollover in 1998, she can pay the $28,000 tax over four years. (For some investors, spreading it out over four years could even lower the tax rate, but not for Cummings.) If we make the same adjustment in the taxable account we set up for her for comparison purposes, the money has less time to grow. With these assumptions, she'll have $101,642 in her taxable account (instead of $112,474) to pay the $100,912 tax bill on the traditional IRA. That will put her only $730 ahead with the traditional IRA rather than $11,562. Cummings may be willing to live with that difference in order to get the increased flexibility of the Roth IRA.

Of course, many other scenarios are possible. It pays to do the computation.

Conversion rollovers may be accomplished by either of the two methods traditionally available for IRA rollovers: the money is sent directly to the custodian of the new IRA or the IRA owner takes a distribution from the old IRA and deposits it in the new IRA within 60 days. All the regular rules apply, including time limits and withholding requirements.

A third method is available as well. An owner of a traditional IRA may convert the existing IRA to a Roth IRA simply by informing the trustee or custodian of the IRA.

Rollovers from One IRA to Another IRA of the Same Type

An IRA owner may withdraw, tax free, all or part of the assets from an IRA if he or she reinvests the assets within 60 days in another IRA. Because this is a rollover, the IRA owner cannot deduct the amount that he or she invests in the new IRA.

For example, suppose Carlos has his IRA in a certificate of deposit (CD) at a bank. Because interest rates are down and the stock market is zooming, Carlos wants to invest the money in a common stock mutual fund. He may withdraw the money from the bank in the form of a check and mail the check to arrive at the mutual fund within 60 days of the withdrawal, completing the rollover.

Carlos should confirm the arrival of his funds at the mutual fund company as early as possible so that any problems with the rollover can be identified and corrected before the 60-day rollover window expires.

Watch the Calendar

If an IRA owner keeps the money rolled over from an IRA in his or her hands longer than the 60-day limit dictated by the IRS, the money becomes ineligible for rollover treatment and must be declared as income.

As stated before, the IRS permits only *one* rollover per account per year. Losing track of the last rollover from a particular IRA account can cause potential problems with the IRS.

Consider this scenario: On April 20, Wanda, who is 40 years old, requests that Lincoln Bank, at which she has an IRA invested in a CD, send her a check for the account when the CD expires. On May 1, Wanda receives a check for $2,500. Wanda spends the money on a vacation, then notices that the First National Bank is offering a 9 percent rate on three-month CDs. Wanda borrows another $2,500 from her sister and starts a CD at First National Bank, telling First National that this is a rollover from Lincoln Bank. Wanda closes the deal June 28, beating the 60-day deadline. She claims this as a rollover. So far, the IRS agrees.

In mid-July, Wanda requests and receives $5,000 from another IRA account at First National. Immediately, she puts the money into an IRA mutual fund account, claiming it as a rollover. On September 28, that three-month CD at First National Bank matures (the one established on June 28). Wanda picks up a check for $2,500 plus $56.25 interest from First National. She consolidates the money with the $5,000 mutual fund account, claiming this as a rollover. This time the IRS does *not* agree.

Why? Wanda already rolled over that $2,500 only a few months earlier from Lincoln to First National. Wanda owes current income taxes on the $2,556.25. She also faces a 10 percent penalty because she is under age 59½.

Wanda's problem might have been avoided had she directly transferred her funds on an institution-to-institution basis. If the bank had transferred the money directly to the mutual fund at Wanda's request, she would technically have made a transfer, not a rollover, with its limit of one permitted per account per year. With a transfer her money would go to her destination just the same, and Wanda doesn't risk breaking the rollover rule.

Inherited IRAs

If an individual inherits an IRA or qualified plan funds from his or her deceased spouse, he or she can generally roll it over into an IRA. If an individual inherits an IRA from someone other than a spouse, he or she can neither roll it over nor allow it to be received as a rollover contribution.

■ ROLLOVERS FROM QUALIFIED PLANS

Thanks to the availability of IRA rollovers, it's possible to postpone the taxation of qualified plan benefits at the time of distribution. This is accomplished by rolling over within 60 days the plan distribution, totally or in part, into an IRA or into another qualified pension or profit-sharing plan. The earnings will then continue to accumulate tax deferred until withdrawals are made.

Only eligible distributions from a taxpayer's (or the taxpayer's deceased spouse) qualified plan may be rolled over entirely or partially into an IRA. The distribution must come from an employer's pension, profit-sharing plan, stock bonus plan, annuity plan or tax-sheltered annuity plan (403(b) plan) that meets the Internal Revenue Code requirements for qualified plans.

An eligible rollover distribution is usually the taxable part of any distribution from a qualified retirement plan, except for a required minimum distribution and any of a series of substantially equal periodic distributions paid at least once a year over (1) the taxpayer's lifetime or life expectancy, (2) the lifetimes or life expectancies of the taxpayer and his or her beneficiary, or (3) a period of 10 years or more.

A *partial rollover* occurs when an employee receives a distribution from a qualified plan and then decides to roll over only a portion of the distribution. The portion retained, of course, must be reported as income; the portion rolled over will remain tax deferred.

Under prior laws, your clients had to roll over at least 50 percent of their distributions in order to continue tax deferral. Since January 1993, a participant can retain any portion of a distribution and then transfer the remaining amount into an IRA rollover or another employer's qualified retirement plan.

ILL. 5.2 ■ *Making Choices*

If an individual has a choice between keeping retirement funds in a company pension plan or in an IRA, he or she is almost always better off choosing the IRA. The IRA provides more flexibility than most company plans. Here are some reasons why:

- *Distributions.* Many company plans offer the participant annuity distributions on a fixed schedule. An IRA gives the participant many more alternatives. Of course, the participant may acquire an annuity contract within the framework of the IRA and thus take the same type of annuity payout (from the IRA) that would generally be available from the typical employer retirement plan.

  However, the participant may be more concerned with continuing to defer taxes than receiving a life income. With an IRA, an individual may take only minimum distributions to keep as much money as possible in the IRA for as long as possible to let tax-deferred investment returns keep growing.

- *Investments.* An IRA lets the participant make almost any type of investment that he or she would like. Because funds left in employer-qualified plans are controlled by the plan trustee, the employee may have limited control over how the funds are invested, or worse, he or she may have no control at all.

- *Withdrawals.* IRA owners can withdraw their money early, even if it means paying a penalty. The decision belongs to them. Qualified plans are much more stringent.

- *Beneficiaries.* Employees are legally required to name their spouses as the beneficiaries of their companies' qualified retirement plans, unless the spouse agrees, in writing, to a different beneficiary.

  However, with an IRA, the participant can name a child or grandchild as the beneficiary so that the child can inherit the account. (The IRA must still be maintained in the deceased IRA owner's name for the benefit of the child.)

- *Security.* Unfortunately, many of today's company pension plans are underfunded. Even if employers and their qualified plans are healthy now, it's risky to assume that such plans will not falter years from now when participants must depend on them for retirement income. With an IRA, participants know that the money is available. It remains under the participant's control.

Withholding Tax on Qualified Plan Rollovers

Employers are required to withhold 20 percent of distributions from a qualified plan unless the employee tells the employer to transfer directly or roll over this amount to an IRA or other qualified plan. This 20 percent withholding rule applies even if the participant completes the rollover within the required 60 days. Note, however, that the full amount of the distribution, including the 20 percent withheld, must be rolled over if the employee wants to avoid all taxes and penalties. This is explained in Ill. 5.3.

A direct rollover may be made by a wire transfer or check mailed to the IRA or a new employer's qualified retirement plan. The IRS is mainly concerned that the check is payable or is transferred directly to the trustee or custodian. It is acceptable to provide the departing employee with a check payable to the trustee of the eligible plan.

ILL. 5.3 ■ *20 Percent Withholding—A Case Study*

Consider the following situation when it comes to the 20 percent withholding requirement.

Peter Connors, age 53, is director of communications for a manufacturing firm. Peter is in the 28 percent marginal income tax bracket. He is to receive $100,000 from his employer's qualified plan. Because he chooses to receive a direct cash distribution personally, he will receive only $80,000. To make the distribution entirely tax free, Peter would have to put an amount equal to the entire distribution—$100,000—into another qualified plan or an IRA. If the missing $20,000 is not included in the rollover amount, it will be treated as taxable.

This means that Peter must roll over the $80,000 and make up the missing $20,000 from his own pocket. Assuming Peter does not have an extra $20,000 available, he will owe income taxes on the withheld $20,000 (20 percent of the total distribution) plus a 10 percent penalty (because he is under 59½). Based on Peter's 28 percent marginal income tax bracket, he will owe $5,600 in regular income tax *plus* an additional $2,000 in early withdrawal penalties, for a combined tax liability of $7,600.

The IRS will return the withheld funds after the employee files a tax return, as long as the full distribution is rolled over within 60 days into another employee plan or IRA. Because the withheld 20 percent is treated as a taxable distribution, the employee will need to make up the withheld 20 percent from his or her own funds to accomplish a 100 percent tax-free rollover. Otherwise, the 20 percent will be treated as taxable. Aside from the income taxes owed on the amount, the employee will also pay a 10 percent penalty if he or she is under age 59½.

The plan making the direct distribution must comply with this requirement. Employees who do not directly rollover and receive distributions themselves will receive only 80 percent of their account because 20 percent will be withheld.

Avoiding the Withholding Tax

To avoid the withholding tax, the participant should request a direct trustee-to-trustee transfer to a new qualified plan or IRA. A direct transfer is the only way to escape the 20 percent withholding requirement. Qualified plans must permit employees who request rollover distributions to elect a direct trustee-to-trustee transfer.

However, if the intent is to roll the funds over to another qualified plan, there is a possibility that the new plan will not accept such transfers. Before a participant makes his or her direct transfer plans, he or she should confirm that the new (transferee) plan will accept the funds directly. Indeed, because of potential recordkeeping problems, many qualified plans won't accept funds from other plans.

The administrator of an employer's qualified plan must provide employees who request a distribution a written explanation (within a reasonable period of time) that must, at a minimum, contain the following information:

- the taxpayer's right to have the distribution paid tax free directly to an IRA or other eligible retirement plan;

- the employer's requirement to withhold tax from the distribution if it is not paid directly to an IRA or other eligible retirement plan;

- the nontaxability of any part of the distribution that is rolled over into an IRA or another eligible retirement plan within 60 days from receipt of the distribution; and

- if applicable, other rules pertaining to the employer's qualified plan, including those for lump-sum distributions, alternate payees in divorce situations and cash or deferred arrangements.

The IRS defines a *reasonable period of time* as "no earlier than 90 days and no later than 30 days before the distribution is made."

Under certain circumstances a participant may need to receive a distribution in less than 30 days after the explanation has been provided. The IRS will allow such distributions as long as both of the following two requirements are met:

1. The employee must have the opportunity to consider whether he or she wants to make a direct rollover for at least 30 days after the explanation is provided.

2. The information sent to the taxpayer must clearly state that he or she has 30 days to make a decision between receiving funds or arranging for a direct rollover.

Plan participants, that is, employees, must also cooperate in the process by providing the plan administrator with timely information about the qualified plan or IRA to which the transfer will be made.

Insurance Contracts

When a participant's qualified plan contains life insurance contracts, transferring into an IRA is probably a poor choice. Although property other than cash may be rolled into an IRA, the Internal Revenue Code specifically disallows the investment of IRA funds in life insurance.

An employee may not transfer a distributed life insurance contract into an IRA. Moreover, the value of the life insurance contract, except for amounts that were considered to have been distributed to the employee, are immediately taxable to the employee.

Keogh to IRA Rollovers

Participants who are self-employed are generally treated as "employees" for rollover purposes. Participants may roll over part or all of a distribution from a Keogh plan into an IRA or other eligible retirement plan.

If the recipient of a distribution from a Keogh plan is under 59½, self-employed and not disabled, any payout from an operating Keogh cannot be treated as a lump-sum distribution, meaning it will not qualify for forward-averaging tax treatment. Thus, a rollover might be an attractive alternative.

Rollovers from Tax-Sheltered Annuities

An eligible distribution from a tax-sheltered annuity (TSA) plan can be rolled over into an IRA or into another tax-sheltered annuity plan. A TSA is a retirement vehicle to meet the needs of employees of certain nonprofit, charitable, education and religious organizations. Contributions to a TSA are excluded from a participant's gross income, and his or her earnings in a TSA accumulate tax free until distributed.

However, a TSA cannot be rolled into another type of retirement plan, such as a qualified pension plan.

Conduit IRAs

When an individual transfers money from a qualified plan and anticipates that he or she might later want to roll those funds into another qualified plan, he or she should set up a *new* IRA to hold the rollover funds rather than mixing them with a previously established IRA. In fact, a participant should establish a new and completely separate rollover account every time he or she leaves a company taking a retirement plan distribution.

Keeping the IRA rollover separate from other IRAs preserves a participant's right to roll that account later into a new employer's plan if the new employer will accept the rollover. An IRA established to receive qualified plan rollovers is generally known as a *conduit IRA*.

Conduit IRAs can be viewed as a temporary holding place for distributions that are received from qualified plans. The purpose of a conduit IRA is to allow the participant to put distributions from qualified plans into a temporary—and tax-sheltered—place until the distributions can be rolled over into another qualified plan.

■ CHAPTER 5 QUESTIONS FOR REVIEW

1. A rollover is generally tax free EXCEPT when it is from

    A. one traditional IRA to another

    B. an employer plan to a traditional IRA

    C. one Roth IRA to another

    D. a traditional IRA to a Roth IRA

2. Which of the following techniques will help a participant avoid the 20 percent withholding associated with distributions from qualified retirement plans?

A. Keeping transfers under $2,000 per year

B. Arranging for a direct trustee-to-trustee transfer

C. Signing a withholding waiver

D. Any of the above

3. In most circumstances, qualified plan assets may NOT be rolled into a traditional IRA if the qualified plan contains

A. life insurance

B. mutual funds

C. cash

D. bonds

4. The tax on a conversion from a traditional IRA to a Roth IRA

A. is spread over four years if the conversion occurs in 1998

B. does not apply if the account was held for five years

C. applies to nondeductible contributions as well as deductible contributions and earnings

D. is equal to 10 percent of the taxable amount

5. An IRA that is a temporary holding place for distributions received from a qualified plan is generally known as a

A. holding IRA

B. temporary IRA

C. conduit IRA

D. partial IRA

6

Other Types of IRAs

T raditional IRAs and Roth IRAs are two sides of the same coin when it comes to retirement planning. Every IRA investor has $2,000 to invest each year in one of these types of IRA. The investor may divide that amount between Roth and traditional IRAs in any way, but the total may not exceed $2,000. A husband and wife may open separate IRAs, but the maximum they can put away in a single year between them is $4,000.

This chapter deals with variations on the IRA concept that allow individuals and married couples to put even more away. These variations include education IRAs, which give parents (and others) modest assistance in saving for a child's education; medical savings accounts; IRAs that are used as part of a simplified employer-sponsored plan; and Keogh plans for the self-employed.

■ ■ ■ ■ ■

■ EDUCATION IRAS

The fact that IRAs are not just for retirement anymore is best exemplified by education IRAs, which may not even be used for retirement. These investment vehicles, which first became available in 1998, are designed for individuals who expect to be paying all or part of the educational expenses for their children or grandchildren.

Annual Contribution Limits

Education IRAs are different from retirement IRAs in that they are set up for someone other than the investor—namely, the child that the investor plans to send to college. Any number of people may contribute to a child's education IRA, but the maximum that may be received from all sources per year is $500 per child under the age of 18. So, if the parents contribute $300, for example, the grandparents are limited to contributing $200.

No tax deduction is allowed for these contributions, but the money is allowed to grow in the education IRA tax free, just like any other type of IRA.

The $500 annual limit is modest, but parents who begin a program for a child born in 1998 could have $25,000 in the account when the child turns 18. Since the $500 limit applies per-child, a family of four could increase their IRA maximum contribution from $4,000 ($2,000 for each parent) to $5,000 (adding $500 for each child).

It is important to note that, while every education IRA may receive up to $500 in contributions per year, upper-income individuals may be prohibited from contributing or may have a lower limit than $500. What does this mean?

There is an income-based phaseout on the contribution limit. For single contributors, the phaseout range is between $95,000 and $110,000. For married contributors filing jointly, the phaseout range is between $150,000 and $160,000. Below the phaseout range, the contributor may make the entire $500 contribution himself. Above the phaseout range, no contribution is allowed.

The fact that one individual is precluded from contributing, however, doesn't mean that someone else will be precluded. If the parents can't contribute, maybe the grandparents can. If the parents are divorced and one parent is phased out, maybe the other parent will be permitted to contribute. Just so long as the total of all contributions to a child's account do not exceed $500 per year.

Let's see how this works:

Carla and Nathan are divorced. Carla earned $104,000 this year and Nathan earned $135,000. Nathan's income exceeds the phaseout range for single taxpayers, so he can't contribute to the education IRA they set up for their daughter Claudia. Carla can, but she may not contribute more than $200. This is computed as follows:

$110,000	Top of AGI phaseout window for single individuals
−104,000	Carla's AGI
$ 6,000	
÷ 15,000	Size of phaseout range
.4	
× $500	Total contribution limit
$200	Carla's maximum contribution

Claudia is not out of luck, however, just because her parents are prohibited from making the full $500 contribution to her education IRA. Her grandparents could make up the difference if their incomes fall below (or within) the phaseout range. Between the various members of the family, Claudia's education IRA still could collect up to $500 per year in contributions until she turns 18.

■ DISTRIBUTIONS MAY BE TAX FREE (AND MAY NOT BE)

Contributing to an education IRA may take a small leap of faith: the child must go to school if distributions are to be received tax free—and no education tax credit may be claimed by the parents in the year of the distribution. Let's look at the education requirement first.

To be tax free, a distribution must be spent on tuition, fees, books, supplies and equipment required for the child's attendance at an eligible educational institution, which includes most accredited post-secondary schools—junior college, college, graduate school and professional school. Distributions may also go toward room and board if the child is in a degree program and carries at least one-half of the normal full-time work load at the particular school.

Payments need not go directly for these expenses, but if the distribution exceeds them in a particular year, the excess is subject to tax under rules discussed later in this chapter. The maximum amount of room and board expense that may be taken into account for this purpose is the amount set by the school for purposes of calculating the cost of attendance for federal financial aid programs. This figure should be available from the school's financial aid office.

Distributions Are Taxable If Education Tax Credit Is Claimed

Distributions that might otherwise be tax free under the rules just described will still be subject to tax if the child or her parents claim an education tax credit based on the education expenses the child incurred during the year. It's an either/or proposition. A credit may be claimed or an education IRA distribution can be received tax free, but not both.

What credits are involved? There are two credits, the Hope Scholarship Credit and the Lifetime Learning Credit:

1. The Hope Scholarship Credit is worth up to $1,500 for each of a child's first two years of post-secondary education. The amount of the credit is 100 percent of the first $1,000 of tuition plus 50 percent of the second $1,000. This is claimed by the parent for a dependent child.

2. The Lifetime Learning Credit is worth 20 percent of the first $5,000 of tuition expenses incurred by anyone in the family (dependents and parents) for a maximum family total of $1,000 per year (this figure doubles in 2004). The Lifetime Learning Credit may not be taken for a child if the Hope credit is taken, but it may be taken for other members of the family.

These credits are phased out at fairly modest income levels. For married couples filing jointly, the phaseout range is $80,000 to $100,000. For others, the phaseout range is $40,000 to $50,000. Individuals with incomes above the phaseout levels don't get the credit, so they don't have to choose between the credit and the tax exclusion for the IRA distribution. They simply take the exclusion.

"Taxable" Distributions

What if your client takes a distribution in the year he or she takes the credit? Or what if the distribution is taken in a year that there are no qualified education expenses or the education expenses are less than the distribution?

The answer is: the distribution is "taxable," but that might not be so bad, even though an additional 10 percent is tacked on to the regular rate for this type of distribution.

ILL. 6.1 ■ *Should a Client's Child Take a Distribution from an Education IRA to Pay for School?*

Tax credit or IRA distribution: that is the question. It's one or the other, but not both. Deciding which would be better is complicated.

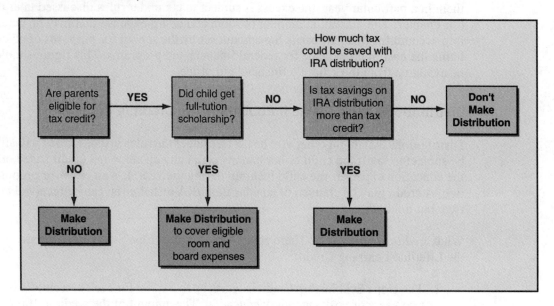

Are Parents Eligible for Tax Credit?
If the parents' income exceeds the phaseout level (the parent claiming the dependency deduction if the parents are divorced), there is no credit and, therefore, no choice to make. A distribution will be tax free as long as it doesn't exceed qualifying educational expenses.

Did Child Get Full-Tuition Scholarship?
If tuition and related expenses are paid for by a scholarship, there's no Hope credit or Lifetime Learning credit, because those credits are limited to tuition and related expenses. If the child has qualifying room-and-board expenses, no credit is available but the distribution will be tax free up to the amount of the expense.

Is the Tax Savings on IRA Distribution More Than the Tax Credit?
If the previous two questions didn't settle it, you have to get out your calculator to determine whether the tax savings on the IRA distribution will be better or worse than that produced by the credit.

You will have to figure out the tax that would be due on a taxable distribution in two ways—one, assuming that it were taken now and, two, assuming that the distribution were delayed to a future year.

To do this, you have to figure the taxable amount—contributions are returned tax free. You have to determine the child's tax bracket and whether the child has deductions to shelter the income (a dependent child doesn't get the regular standard deduction). Finally, you have to add a 10 percent penalty tax—10 percent of the taxable portion only. After all is said and done, the effective tax rate on the distribution could be zero or quite low. The client might be better off taking the credit and paying the tax on the distribution. But with a low tax like that, the IRA has done its job.

The reasons why a taxable distribution might not be so bad are as follows.

- The contributions themselves are paid out tax free. Only the earnings are taxed. This is like a nondeductible traditional IRA (which is discussed in greater detail in Chapter 4). What this means is that only a fraction of the distribution is really subject to tax.

- College students are typically in the lowest tax bracket, which is now 15 percent (but may not be 15 percent in the future when distributions from today's education IRAs are taken). Add on 10 percent and the student is paying 25 percent, which is not great but may be better than what the parents are paying in tax.

- If the child is old enough that he or she is no longer a dependent of the parents, he or she can shelter up to $6,950 (1998 figures) in regular tax if he or she is single because of the standard deduction and personal exemption. In that case, only the 10 percent tax applies. (If the child is not a dependent, however, the parents may not claim an education tax credit for him or her.)

Let's see how this works.

Kathy Hagen, age 22, graduates college in May 2006 and doesn't continue on to graduate or professional school. She paid for her last year of college in the fall of 2005, so she had no qualified education expenses in 2006. Kathy gets an apartment of her own when she finds a job in November. She earns only $5,500 for the year.

Kathy's parents started contributing to an education IRA for their daughter in 1998 and continued until she turned 18 (when contributions are no longer allowed). Total contributions were $2,500. They never took a distribution while Kathy was in college because they preferred to take the education credit while they could. In 2006 the account was worth $5,600. She decides to take the whole amount out during the year.

Her tax is $310 on the distribution. The taxable portion of the distribution is $3,100. Add this to the $5,500 she earned on the job to give her an adjusted gross income of $8,600. The standard deduction and personal exemptions grew since 1997 to $8,850. After these deductions, her taxable income is zero. She still owes the 10 percent additional tax, however, which is the $310 dollars.

Kathy's age group will be one of the first withdrawing significant amounts from education IRAs. Larger and larger withdrawals will become possible as time passes, allowing for larger accumulations. Eighteen years of maximum contributions (from birth through age 17) will total $9,000. For children born in 1998, this total will be reached in 2015. Earnings could bring the total account value to $25,000 or more. And the child could hold the account for up to 12 years more (without new contributions) as there is an indication that accounts will have to be distributed by age 30. (This is stated in congressional committee reports. The limit is not found in the Tax Code, however.)

Rollovers and Transfers to Another Beneficiary

Like other IRAs, education IRAs may be rolled over so that investors may change investment vehicles without paying tax. A distribution for this purpose must be reinvested in the new education IRA within 60 days and only one rollover is allowed per year.

Unlike other IRAs, education IRAs may be transferred from one owner to another. If one child does not use his or her education IRA or leaves part of it unused, the account may be transferred to another member of the family. The circle of family members that may receive the transfer include the child's brothers and sisters, the child's own children, the child's parents (the people who may have set up the IRA in the first place), aunts and uncles, nieces and nephews, and spouses of any of these.

The effect of this rule is that education IRAs can be used to create a kind of general education fund for families. Contributions may be made only on behalf of children under the age of 18, but through the mechanism of transfer, the money can be spent for the education of other family members.

Parents who are uncertain whether a particular child will go to college don't have to worry that the tax benefits of that child's education IRA will be lost if the decision is negative. The money can simply be passed on to another family member. And if the other family members are significantly younger, the money has longer to compound tax free.

■ MEDICAL SAVINGS ACCOUNTS

Medical Savings Accounts (MSAs) are another variant of the IRA concept designed primarily to assist your client with medical bills, but they can provide important benefits at retirement if you client and his or her family stay healthy.

You should be aware that MSAs are available now in a pilot program scheduled to last from 1997 through 2000. Only 750,000 accounts may be opened nationally and only self-employed individuals and employees of small employers (50 or fewer employees at the time the employer chooses to participate) may participate.

Another requirement of the program is that participating individuals and their families must be covered by "high-deductible" health insurance. This is defined as follows:

- For individual coverage, the minimum deductible is $1,500, the maximum deductible is $2,250, and the maximum out-of-pocket limitation is $3,000.

- For family coverage, the minimum deductible is $3,000, the maximum deductible is $4,500, and the maximum out-of-pocket limitation is $5,500.

These amounts will be adjusted for inflation after 1998.

The idea of the MSA-insurance combination is that routine medical bills will be paid out of the MSA and catastrophic medical bills will be paid by insurance. So where does retirement come in? Let's look at how the MSA works.

MSAs and Retirement Savings

An MSA is like a combination of the best features of a traditional IRA and a Roth IRA:

- Contributions are deductible (or employer contributions to the account are not taxed).

- Earnings are not taxed.

- Withdrawals for medical expenses are not taxed.

- Distributions may be taken for any purpose at the individual's regular tax rate after he or she becomes eligible for Medicare (currently age 65).

Early distributions not used for medical expenses are subject to a 15 percent penalty in addition to income tax. Participants are not required to get sick or, if they do get sick, to spend money from the MSA. Anything left in the account becomes a retirement fund.

One last point will complete the picture—the amount that may be contributed each year:

- For individuals, contributions are limited to 65 percent of the annual deductible in the individual's health coverage. Based on the restrictions on deductibles noted above, the maximum annual contribution will fall between $975 and $1,462.50.

- For family coverage, contributions are limited to 75 percent of the annual deductible. Based on the restrictions noted above, the maximum annual contribution will fall between $2,250 and $3,375.

Medicare+Choice MSAs

Beginning in 1999 another pilot program will begin to allow seniors (Medicare eligible) to open MSAs in conjunction with a new type of high-deductible Medicare coverage. Under the pilot program, 390,000 Medicare Plus Choice MSAs will be allowed nationwide.

Medicare+Choice MSAs are similar to regular MSAs in operation except for two points:

1. Contributions are made by the federal government (since the Medicare+Choice MSA program is an alternative to regular Medicare coverage, which the federal government pays for).

2. A stiff penalty (50 percent in addition to tax) applies to "excess" withdrawals for purposes other than qualified medical expenses of the accountholder. Medical expenses for spouse or dependents don't count.

Withdrawals for medical expenses of the accountholder are tax free. Withdrawals made upon death or disability are taxed, but the 50 percent penalty does not apply.

ILL. 6.2 ■ *How an MSA Can Supplement a Retirement Program*

Stuart Cushman was 42 in 1997, married and self-employed. He opened an MSA in 1997 and switched his health coverage to a high-deductible plan that had a $3,000 deductible. He made the maximum contributions to the MSA, which were $2,250 per year (75 percent of $3,000). In the process of switching insurance, Cushman saved $2,000 in premium costs. High-deductible policies are cheaper than low-deductible. After figuring in tax savings, his overall costs were about the same as before he opened the MSA.

Cushman and his family were healthy, but they got sick now and then. In the first 10 years, medical expenses for him, his wife and his two children varied between $1,500 and $2,000 a year. Then his kids went off on their own and medical expenses dropped to between $1,000 and $1,500 per year. Since his medical expenses were considerably less than his annual contributions, the account started to grow.

When Cushman turned 65 in 2020, the account held $65,000. If he withdrew the money in the 28 percent tax bracket, he'd have $46,800 after taxes.

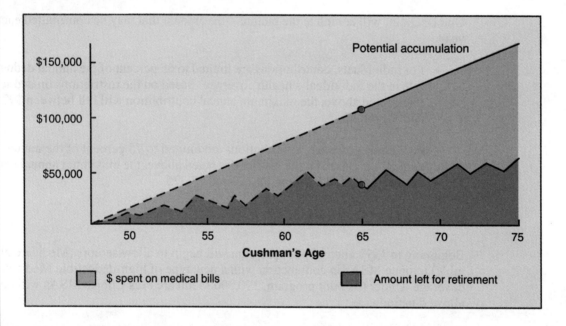

Cushman's cost for health coverage went down when he switched to the MSA program. (Remember, although the MSA contribution was slightly higher than the insurance premium, he also had a deductible to pay under the old plan.) Yet, he ended up with $46,800 to spend at retirement—all this for a negative investment!

Of course, Cushman was lucky. Some people do get sick and will use all the money in their MSA for medical expenses. But if the medical expenses get too large, the insurance will kick in, preventing significant loss. You can't rely on an MSA for retirement, but there's a significant upside potential—and little risk of loss.

So more than the regular MSA, Medicare+Choice MSAs are restricted to medical expenses. Nevertheless, seniors can augment their savings with this type of account if their medical expenses are low.

■ KEOGHS FOR THE SELF-EMPLOYED

Self-employed individuals have a choice: they can open IRAs or they can set up their own qualified retirement plan, known as a Keogh. Keoghs are not IRAs and the rules covering them are way beyond the scope of this course. But, for a business owner, they are an important alternative. Here are some pros and cons you should know:

- Contribution limits are much higher for Keoghs than for IRAs. Contributions to a Keogh can be as high as $30,000 per year (depending on income) compared to $2,000. (Contributions may be even higher in some circumstances with some pension-type Keoghs.)

- If the business owner has employees, they must be covered by the plan. This could mean additional payroll expense, but it need not. It depends on the type of plan. A simple 401(k) Keogh merely allows employees to contribute, but the contribution maximum drops to $10,000 (in 1998) and special rules apply to ensure participation of all employees.

- Keogh plans may allow participants (both the owner and employees) to borrow from their accounts. As we've seen, IRAs allow restricted preretirement withdrawals for home purchases and medical and education expenses, but there is no mechanism for replenishing the retirement fund. Keoghs allow a participant to borrow the funds when needed (for any purpose) and to repay them.

- Keogh plans entail significantly more paperwork and compliance than an IRA—although Keogh plan providers may simplify this by offering standardized plans.

■ IRAs AS PART OF AN EMPLOYER PLAN

Employers who don't want the complexity of a full-blown qualified retirement plan may use IRAs as part of a simplified retirement plan. There are two ways this is done: the SIMPLE-IRA and the SEP-IRA.

SIMPLE-IRA. SIMPLE stands for **S**avings **I**ncentive **M**atch **PL**ans for **E**mployees. A small business with 100 or fewer employees may be entitled to set up a SIMPLE plan. Plans may be structured like a 401(k) plan or in the form of a traditional IRA. Regular IRA limits don't apply, however.

Employees may make elective contributions of up to $6,000 per year. Employers are required to match employee contributions up to 3 percent of compensation or make nonelective contributions to employee accounts of 2 percent of compensation.

Employees can't decide to set up SIMPLE-IRAs but if the employer offers them, they may have a choice whether to participate. An employee given this choice may be able to put more money away in the SIMPLE-IRA than in a regular IRA.

SEP-IRA. SEP stands for **S**implified **E**mployee **P**ension. Under a SEP, an employer contributes to traditional IRAs for each employee. Regular IRA contribution limits don't apply. Instead, employer contributions are limited to 15 percent of compensation or $24,000, whichever is less. ($30,000 is the legal limit but in most cases only $160,000 of compensation may be taken into account. Fifteen percent of $160,000 is $24,000.)

Although the higher contribution limit is attractive, SEP plans are subject to complicated nondiscrimination rules that don't apply to SIMPLE plans and *certainly* don't apply to IRAs.

▪ CHAPTER 6 QUESTIONS FOR REVIEW

1. All of the following represent differences between a Keogh plan and an IRA EXCEPT

   A. Keogh plans must provide benefits for the owner's employees

   B. Investment earnings in a Keogh are not taxed until withdrawn

   C. Contribution limits are significantly higher for a Keogh

   D. Keogh plans may allow the participant to borrow

2. Distributions from an education IRA are tax free if

   A. contributions were deducted on the parent's tax return

   B. they are taken after the child has reached age 18

   C. they are spent for education and no education tax credit is claimed

   D. they are spent for education regardless of whether the education tax credit is claimed or not

3. How does an MSA contribute to a retirement savings program?

   A. Withdrawals for medical expenses are not taxed.

   B. Earnings in the account are not taxed.

   C. Contributions are deductible (or employer contributions to the account are not taxed).

   D. Any remaining account balance may be distributed without penalty after the owner reaches age 65.

4. How does a SIMPLE-IRA differ from a traditional IRA?

   A. Contributions by employers to SIMPLE-IRAs may exceed $2,000 per year.

   B. Earnings on investments in a SIMPLE-IRA are not taxed.

   C. Withdrawals from SIMPLE-IRAs are taxable.

   D. All of the above

5. Accountholders may make tax-free rollovers to an account held for the benefit a different person only in the case of the following

A. Medical Savings Account

B. Roth IRA

C. Education IRA

D. Keogh plan

Answer Key to Questions for Review

CHAPTER 1
1. B
2. B
3. C
4. B
5. C

CHAPTER 2
1. D
2. B
3. A
4. D
5. B

CHAPTER 3
1. C
2. A
3. B
4. A
5. C

CHAPTER 4
1. D
2. C
3. D
4. C
5. B

CHAPTER 5
1. D
2. B
3. A
4. A
5. C

CHAPTER 6
1. B
2. C
3. D
4. A
5. C